An Insider's
SECRETS
To Becoming A Flight Attendant

By
Luauna Rule

Flight Attendant Corporation of America
Denver, Colorado

An Insider's
SECRETS
To Becoming A Flight Attendant

by Luauna Rule

Published by:

Flight Attendant Corporation Of America
Post Office Box 260803
Littleton, Colorado 80163-9961

Library of Congress Catalog Card Number: 97-90017
ISBN: 0-96564-384-0

Warning- Disclaimer

This publication provides the Author's opinion in regards to the subject matter. This publication is designed to provide accurate and authoritative information in regards to the subject matter covered. There may, however, be errors of content or typography and the Author makes no guarantee, warranties or representations of any kind. It is sold with the understanding that the author is not engaged in rendering legal or professional service or advice of any kind . This book is in no way a guarantee of employment.

Contents

Introduction i

PART 1 - How To Know If A Flight Attendant Career Is For You
    Chapter 1 - The 90's Flight Attendant.................................... 1
    Chapter 2 - A Typical Day... 7
    Chapter 3 - What Are The Airlines Looking For In A Flight Attendant? 11

PART 2 - How To Chose The Best Employer For You
    Chapter 4 - Types Of Carriers... 21

PART 3 - How To Present Yourself In The Most Impressive Way
    Throughout The Application Process
    Chapter 5 - General Guidelines... 33
    Chapter 6 - The Cover Letter.. 37
    Chapter 7 - The Resume.. 45
    Chapter 8 - The Application.. 55

PART 4 - How To Conquer The Interviewing Process
    Chapter 9 - Interviewing - The Basic Do's and Don'ts......... 65
    Chapter 10- Types of Interviews... 73
    Chapter 11- The Most Commonly Asked Interview Questions............ 83

PART 5 - How To Survive Training
    Chapter 12 - Training Program Outline................................. 93
    Chapter 13 - What Training Is _Really_ Like.......................... 99

Reference
    Airline Directory.. 100
    Job Log... 113
    Military Conversion Chart... 114
    Airline City Codes.. 115
    Fact Sheets On The Major Carriers.................................... 116
    Additional Sources Of Information..................................... 126
    Glossary.. 127

Introduction

So you're considering joining the friendly skies! A career as a flight attendant is one of the most exciting and rewarding careers available, offering incredible travel benefits as well as a great deal of flexibility and freedom. Coming from someone who has been a flight attendant for both a major and regional airline, I would have to say you have made an excellent decision. Working as a flight attendant is not only a great way to travel on someone else's tab, but an incredibly fun job that offers a great deal of variety and freedom.

Unfortunately for those attempting to get hired with the airlines, I am not the only one who feels this way. Because of the unique benefits inherent in only this position, the airlines are inundated with thousands of requests each day. The lure of a sensational career that offers the opportunity to see the world for free, brings many more qualified applicants to the field than the airlines are able to accommodate. The doors are open to so many more applicants today, versus years ago when flight attendants had to be single young females. The flight attendant position is perfect for a variety of individuals: those who are trying to escape the daily grind of a dead end job, recent college graduates looking for adventure, individuals seeking a flexible schedule and travel opportunities, people with grown children looking to enter the workforce, etc. Now that this incredible career opportunity is accessible to more people, it means much stronger competition for the positions available.

I began my flight attendant search years ago, fresh out of college with very little knowledge of the airline industry. I was in for quite a surprise when I began the application process. First, I wasn't even sure how to begin my search. Second, I didn't realize how stiff the competition was, and how "unprepared" I really was. Third, I didn't know flight attendant interviews were unlike "normal" interviews, and therefore required special preparation. Needless to say, I was pretty ignorant concerning the whole process, and a little overwhelmed and shocked by the "strange world of becoming a flight attendant." I wasted a great deal of valuable time and made costly errors stemming from my lack of knowledge.

The good news is, you don't have to make these same mistakes! This guide is the result of hundreds of hours of research, combined with my personal experience, the experience and wisdom of other flight attendants, along with input from flight attendant supervisors and trainers. The more knowledge you have pertaining to the flight attendant position and unique hiring process, the better equipped you will be to decide if this is the right career choice for you and how to actually go about obtaining a flight attendant position.

After completing this guide you will have a wealth of knowledge that will give you a strong advantage over the competition. Unlike the other applicants, you will know what the airlines look for when hiring flight attendants, for whom you would like to work, how to present yourself in the most impressive way throughout the interviewing process, how to answer the questions you will be asked during the "unique" airline interviews, and how to make it through training with flying colors. You will also have the names and addresses of over 50 potential employers, as well as job hot line numbers with the most current hiring information. You will be given step-by-step instructions, guiding you from beginning to end, and you will be able to begin a thorough and organized job search **immediately** after completion. Everything you need to know is included in this comprehensive step-by-step guide, with **inside tips** not found in any other book. The sooner you get started, the closer you are to an enriching career that offers excitement, travel, and freedom. Good luck!

PART I

How To Know
If A Flight Attendant
Career Is For You

Chapter 1

The 90's Flight Attendant

The flight attendant profession originated back in 1930, although they were referred to then as "stewardesses". United Airlines thought it would be a good idea to hire nurses to tend to their passengers needs, making their customer's flying experience more comfortable. What started as just an added service by one airline over 65 years ago, has grown into the chosen profession of over 100,000 individuals today.

The stereotype of the young, wild "stewardess" of year's past has been replaced with today's more professional, career oriented "flight attendant". It wasn't that long ago when an applicant had to be female, single, and under 27 to work as a "stewardess." A 1995 study conducted by the Association of Flight Attendants, in which a sampling of 600 flight attendants were interviewed, shows just how drastically things have changed over the years. A surprising 43% of flight attendants surveyed were over 40 years of age, 40% had dependent children, 59% were married, and 16% were male. The more gender free job title of "flight attendant" soon replaced "stewardess", when men began entering the field.

There has also been a shift in the way flight attendants view their positions; no longer as just a short term job but as a long term career. The same study showed 51% of flight attendants had worked for their employer more than a decade, 32% for more than 20 years, and fewer than 14% for less than 5 years. An unbelievable 73% are committed to remaining with their present employer until <u>retirement</u>! These statistics, combined with the low turnover rate in the industry, are an excellent representation of the high degree of satisfaction and commitment the majority of flight attendants have regarding their careers.

Although most flight attendants love their jobs and could not imagine doing anything else, like any other career, it's not for everyone. As with any job, there are unique pros and cons related to the position. I will highlight some of the positive and negative attributes of a flight attendant position so you are able to make an educated decision whether this is a career you would enjoy.

Travel Benefits

Probably the most appealing and envied benefit of a flight attendant position are the incredible travel benefits. Not only do you get to tour the cities in which you have layovers, but you are also able to travel on your own carrier (on a space available basis for a nominal charge). Some airlines require their employees to work 3-6 months before they are eligible for travel benefits, although others offer them immediately. If you work for a smaller carrier that does not fly to your desired destinations, you can receive a discount of 75-90% off of most other carriers. You also receive substantial discounts on hotel rooms, car rentals, and cruises -- all just by showing your airline ID! These discounts apply to your spouse, dependents, and usually your parents. Your parents will threaten to take you out of the will if you ever quit! Most airlines also offer "Buddy Passes" which you can give to friends, significant others, and anyone else who does not already receive travel benefits, so they may also travel with you.

Independence

Another unique benefit that often lures people to the job is the independence it provides. Flight attendants don't have a boss looking over their shoulders. If you've ever worked for a difficult boss, you'll understand what an incredible bonus this really is! Each flight attendant is assigned a supervisor; however, it is only necessary to meet with them under special circumstances (i.e. six month review, incident on a flight, etc.). They feel you are an adult and are responsible for knowing what your job is, where you need to be, and when.

Variety

When working as a flight attendant, you will no longer deal with the monotony associated with working 9 to 5. Each day offers something new regarding the places you will see and the people with which you will interact. One day you may be enjoying a bagel for breakfast in New York City, and find yourself having dinner the next evening at the Hard Rock Cafe in London!

Most of the people you come in contact with will have an incredibly positive impact on your life. You will help people celebrate their 50th wedding anniversary, toast honeymooners on their way to Hawaii, transport professional sports teams on their way to the "big game", and even meet the occasional movie star. Of all the wonderful people you will meet, some of the most interesting and memorable will be your own crew members. You will work with people from all over the world, all with interesting backgrounds to share and stories to tell. You may all be very diverse but you all share something in common, which is the desire to travel and experience the world around you.

Most individuals will begin their airline career on reserve. The reserve system covers scheduled trips on a last minute basis, filling in for those calling in sick, flight attendants on vacation, crews missing their connections due to weather and mechanical delays, etc. In most cases, approximately 20% of the base is on reserve. The amount of time you will spend on reserve will depend on a variety of factors, including how quickly a company is hiring and the size of the base. While on reserve, you will be given a schedule for the month with a set number of days off and a set number of days "on call". You cannot be contacted to work on your days off; however, during your "on call" days you can be called to work at any time for any trip.

Being on reserve can be challenging, but it also has its benefits. Most airlines have a guaranteed minimum. This means you are paid a specific amount, whether you work the minimum number of hours for that particular month or not. There were many days I was relaxing by the pool (beeper in hand) on my "call days" and was not needed. I was still being paid my guaranteed minimum for the month, whether I worked or not.

Also, you may not be senior enough to get a trip with a Honolulu layover for years, but senior flight attendants get sick too. On reserve, basking on Kanapali Beach is very possible. I loved it because I was able to see the entire United States, having layovers in all the major cities I had always wanted to visit.

In addition, some carriers have a maximum number of hours you are able to work in a month. Once that maximum point is reached, you are released for the duration of the month. You may work like a maniac for the first part of the month, but it is a wonderful bonus to have an extra ten days off at the end of the month to play!

Flexibility

Most schedules offer a <u>minimum</u> of 12-15 days off a month, which is plenty of time to take advantage of all those great benefits! You "bid" for your schedules on a month to month basis. This means you would list the schedules you would like in order of preference, along with all the other flight attendants. The schedules are awarded based strictly on seniority, with the most senior flight attendant getting his/her first choice, the second most senior getting his/her first choice (unless it is the same as the most senior flight attendant, and then he/she gets their second choice), and so on. You can see why your choices will be more limited when you first begin your career at the bottom of the totem pole, but will increase as your seniority increases.

You can vary your schedule each month depending on your commitments for that particular month. You can choose trips with later check-ins if you are a night person. You can bid for weekends off to spend time with family and friends who have a more traditional schedule. You can request days off during the week for attending school, etc. Changes can be made after you have received your schedule for the month, simply by trading with other flight attendants for more/fewer hours, different days off, different layover spots, etc. Due to the great amount of flexibility and free time flight attendants have, it is very common for them to run their own businesses on the side! Some airlines also allow line sharing, which means two flight attendants share one schedule for the month. This is great for individuals with children, or those who want additional time off for outside interests. Some airlines also offer "buddy bidding", which allows two flight attendants to have the exact same schedule for the month (same trips, same days off). This works out great for friends, as well as couples who fly together.

With additional seniority, you will no longer be "on reserve", but will become a "line holder". This means you will not only be able to "bid" for your preferred days off, but also for the desired trips and layovers you would like. Once again, the more senior you are, the better schedule you will be able to receive. Also, with seniority your pay <u>increases</u> as the number of days you work <u>decrease</u>. It is not uncommon for a senior flight attendant with a major carrier to make over $50,00 a year -- not bad for 12 days of work in a given month! If this sounds too good to be true, it's only fair we also discuss some of the negatives of the position as well.

Instability

I've discussed the great deal of variety this job entails, which may be a challenge for individuals who desire stability. As was stated earlier, most individuals start out on reserve. Normally you will have ample time to prepare for a trip, although there are circumstances where the minimum call out time is given. This can be as little as two hours, so it is sometimes necessary to live fairly close to the airport when first beginning your career.

A flight attendant career may not be the ideal job for those craving a routine schedule. Most trips require flight attendants to be away from home anywhere from one day to over a week at a time, depending on the schedule and the type of carrier. When you first begin your flight attendant career, you may be spending holidays and weekends away from home due to your low seniority. You will also be required to work a variety of hours, varying from very early mornings to very late evenings. Being flexible is <u>extremely</u> important in this position.

Challenging Situations

Although most of the people you come in contact with will be very personable and polite, there are always a few bad apples (intoxicated passengers, aggressive individuals, etc.) If you don't feel you would enjoy working with the general public on a daily basis, you probably would not enjoy a flight attendant career.

Also flight attendants are accepting a certain amount of personal risk on a daily basis, as minimal as it may be, to ensure passenger safety first and foremost. Most people are unaware that **a flight attendant's main responsibility is the safety of the passengers** and any other services that the airline offers are secondary. This is also something that must be considered when pursuing a flight attendant career.

This chapter gives the general drawbacks as well as the benefits of this position. All jobs have both. If you ask any flight attendant they will probably tell you the positives far outweigh the negatives, making it one of the greatest jobs in the world! Read on for an even better idea of what a "typical day" is like (if there is such a thing!) for a flight attendant .

Notes

Chapter 2

A Typical Day

One of the most common questions asked by airlines when interviewing for a flight attendant position is "What are the duties of a flight attendant?". Many people have misconceptions about a day in the life of a flight attendant. Although it may seem that their only responsibilities are to stand around looking like Ken and Barbie, throwing in the occasional "Hi, how are you?" or "Bye Bye", there is a great amount of work involved behind the scenes. The more you know about the position, the more educated you will appear during the interviewing process.

So let's say you are a new flight attendant on reserve, based in Washington, DC. You are "On Call" for six days starting tomorrow, and you just received a call from crew scheduling. They have assigned you the following three day trip, starting tomorrow morning:

	Day 1 Report time	710
#321	IAD-CVG	0825-0940
	CVG-DEN	1015-1050
#432	DEN-SFO	1200-1330
	RON SFO	

	Day 2 Report time	1530
#546	SFO-DEN	1645-2015
	DEN-LAX	2100-2225
	RON LAX	

	Day 3 Report Time	1000
#654	LAX-DFW	1115-1545
	DFW-IAD	1700-2115

Let's review the first day to give you an idea of how to read the schedule. On Day 1 you will check in at 7:10 AM, one hour and fifteen minutes prior to departure (which is usually standard), for flight #321 departing at 8:25 AM to Cincinnati. You will have 35 minutes in Cincinnati before departing for Denver at 10:15 AM on the same flight number. You will have one hour and forty-five minutes in Denver, leaving at 12:00 PM on flight #432 and arriving in San Francisco at 1330 (or 1:30 PM). San Francisco is your scheduled RON (short for "remain overnight") or layover. You are done for the day and free to eat as much Fisherman's Wharf crab or Ghiradelli chocolate as you can take!

On your layovers the airline will provide lodging, transportation to and from the airport, and a per diem allowance for meal expenses. Just make sure you are back for your check-in at 1530 (or 3:30 PM) the next day! Layovers can range from 9-36 hours domestically and even longer internationally. You will usually have ample time to tour the city. If you don't have a long layover on one trip, chances are you'll be back again with a longer layover the next time.

All scheduling in the airline industry is given in military time and all airports are referred to by city codes. You will be tested on military time and city codes at training. You may also be tested on military time during the interviewing process. A military time conversion chart, as well as a list of some of the city codes, is included in the Reference section of this guide.

Now that we have covered scheduling, let's discuss what happens between the time you leave your house for the airport and the time you are eating crab in San Francisco (otherwise referred to as work!). You must check in at your scheduled time, check your mailbox for any correspondence, and find your crew for a "briefing". During the briefing, the First Flight Attendant (also referred to as a Lead Flight Attendant or Purser) will review the trip information as we did above. The First Flight Attendant is in charge of the communication, organization, and coordination between the crew (flight attendants and pilots) on the trip. They will usually be assigned this position based on seniority or by specifically bidding for it, and will receive premium pay for the additional responsibility and paperwork involved. The First Flight Attendant will also assign each crew member certain responsibilities, such as where on the aircraft they will sit, what exits and emergency equipment they are responsible for, and what their responsibilities are during boarding and the in-flight service. They will also notify you of any special circumstances on the trip, such as passengers requiring oxygen, wheelchair passengers, law enforcement officers who may be carrying a weapon, etc.

Once that is completed, all crew members will board the aircraft and check their emergency equipment, making sure everything is functional and air worthy. Then each crew member takes his or her place for their boarding responsibilities, such as galley preparation, ticket taking, greeting passengers, monitoring the size of carry-on baggage (a.k.a. Bag Hag), or helping out passengers in the cabin.

Once the passengers have all boarded the aircraft and the captain has given his approval to shut the door, a safety demonstration is given. One flight attendant makes the announcement over the public address system, while the other flight attendants demonstrate the safety equipment on the aircraft. Although you may feel like a Vanna White wannabe, this is required by the Federal Aviation Administration (GOD in the airline industry). Some of the larger aircraft offer pre-taped videos of the safety demonstration, saving you from this task. The safety demonstration is actually an extremely important part of the flight, as passengers are being educated on how to deal with potential emergency situations. After flight attendants check the cabin and make sure all passengers are in compliance with FAA requirements (seat backs and dining trays in the upright and locked position, arm rests down, seat belts securely fastened, carry-on baggage stowed) they go to their jump seats for take-off.

Once in flight you will begin your in-flight beverage / meal service and tend to the passenger's needs (interacting with the passengers, distributing pillows and blankets, helping unaccompanied minors, calming nervous fliers, etc.) for the duration of the flight. This is when you discover your parents didn't really name you Julie but "Oh Miss". In preparation for landing, you will once again make sure all passengers are complying with FAA requirements and take your jump seat for landing. If this was the first segment of the trip (referred to as a leg) you would then deplane the passengers and prepare for the next leg. If this was your last leg of the trip, you would be right behind the last passenger maximizing your layover time!

If this sounds like a job you would enjoy, continue on to find out exactly what the airlines are looking for in a flight attendant!

Notes

Chapter 3

What Are The Airlines Looking For In A Flight Attendant?

Flight attendants come from all walks of life, bringing to the job a variety of educational training, employment histories, and cultural backgrounds. Although the airlines strive for diversity in their in-flight work force, each carrier has some very specific minimum requirements concerning age, height/weight, vision, and education. The chart on the following page lists the major carriers and their **minimum requirements** for each of these categories. To qualify as a major carrier an airline must generate over 1 billion dollars in annual sales.

If you do not meet these minimums, don't worry. These are just the minimum requirements for the **major** airlines. The regional, charter, and commuter airlines (listed in the Airline Directory found in the Reference section and discussed further in Chapter 4) often have less stringent minimum requirements. Also, these minimums are correct as of the date of this publication. Airlines have been known to change their minimum age, as well as height and weight requirements. If you are set on working for a particular carrier and do not meet their minimums as noted in this guide, please feel free to contact the carrier to verify whether or not the requirements have changed.

Company	Age	Height/ Weight	Vision	Education
Alaska	21	5'2" min *	no requirements	HS diploma or equivalent
America West	20	no set min or max ht *	no requirements	HS diploma or equivalent- 2 yrs college / cust. service
American	20	5'2"-6'0" *	20/50 corrected	HS diploma or equivalent
Continental	20	5'0"-6'2" *	20/30 corrected 20/200 uncorrected	HS diploma or equivalent
Delta	21	no set min or max ht *	no requirements	HS diploma or equivalent
Northwest	18	5'2" min *	20/40 corrected	HS diploma- 2 yrs college / cust. service
Southwest	20	*	20/40 corrected	HS diploma or equivalent
Trans World Airlines	18	chart given at interview	20/50 corrected 20/200 uncorrected	HS diploma or equivalent
United	19	5'2"-6' *	20/30 corrected 20/200 uncorrected / contact 20/100 uncorrected / glasses	HS diploma or equivalent - foreign language
US Air	21	no set min or max ht *	no requirements	HS diploma or equivalent

* weight in proportion to height

Minimum Age

The major carriers are extremely stringent concerning their age minimums. I knew of a 20 year old girl who actually made it all the way through the last week of training, only to be released when they discovered she was not 21. You will be asked to provide proof of your age at some point, so it is best to be honest up front. If you are convinced you want to work for a particular carrier and are under their specified age limit, you have several options. You can attempt to work for the carrier in another capacity, such as a reservation or ticket agent. You can also spend the next few years making yourself more marketable by furthering your education, learning a foreign language and gaining customer service experience. Age minimums for the other types of carriers range from 18-21.

Although there are minimum age requirements, there is not a maximum and you can **not** be discriminated against based upon your age. If you feel you may be too old to start a career as a flight attendant, think again! As noted in the previous chapter, there is a wide age range for flight attendants with the majority of the work force over age 35. Airlines really do hire flight attendants of all ages. There were quite a few people in both of my training classes that were in their forties and fifties, just starting their flight attendant careers.

Height/Weight

The dreaded height/weight charts! Many of the airlines used to have specific height/weight charts that they would follow very strictly, which was unfortunate due to the variety of body types, varying degrees of muscle mass, etc. There are still some airlines that utilize these charts; however, most carriers simply state they are looking for applicants with "weight proportionate to height". This is a touchy area due to recent lawsuits, and all I can recommend is to keep yourself in good shape. If a carrier does have specific height/weight requirements, you will usually be notified of them prior to the interview. If you fall outside their guidelines, try to postpone the interview until you are within their requirements. Otherwise, you will risk losing the interview, and you will have to wait for at least six months to reapply (not to mention the waste of your time and the unnecessary blow to the ego). For some airlines it is not a one time "weigh-in", as your weight may also be monitored during training and at set intervals once you are a working flight attendant.

The reasons for the "weight in proportion to height" requirement is not simply for aesthetic purposes. In the unlikely event of an emergency, a flight attendant has to be able to move through the exits and aisles quickly and easily, as well as manipulate the heavy emergency windows and doors. The daily requirements of a flight attendant position can also be physically challenging. Flight attendants are basically on their feet all day. On any given a day a flight attendant may have to push a heavy service cart up and down the aisle numerous times, lift and manipulate heavy baggage, pass out and pick up hundreds of meals, not to mention all the less strenuous duties performed in what could end up being a 14 hour day. A flight attendant position would be very difficult for someone in poor physical condition.

The major carriers are as stringent on height as they are weight, and unfortunately this is not an area that is controllable. This actually does serve a purpose, as the airlines feel it is a great advantage to have flight attendants that can reach the overhead bins yet are not scraping their head on the ceiling of the cabin! Some airlines actually use a reach test instead of measuring individuals height, usually requiring that the applicants be able to reach at least 75". For those individuals who do not fit into the major carriers strict guidelines, once again you may want to consider working for a regional, charter, or commuter carrier. Commuter airlines actually prefer shorter candidates, as they can move more easily through the smaller cabins.

Education

All the major airlines require a minimum of a high school education or its equivalent (GED). Any additional education is to your advantage, as most carriers would like to see some college, and would prefer a college degree. If you do not have a college degree however, it does not mean you will not get hired. The same survey done by the Association of Flight Attendants mentioned earlier showed that only 29% of flight attendants surveyed had a college degree. Keep in mind you are being hired for your ability to deal with the general public, not your ability to calculate statistical equations!

It is my opinion that the one thing you definitely **do not** need is training from an "airline training school." Although these programs are very useful if you want to become a reservations agent, you do not need that type of training to become a flight attendant. You will be given formal training by the particular carrier once you are hired. In all my years of experience, I have never met a flight attendant who had attended one of these programs. From the knowledge I've been able to gather, no preference is given to graduates of these programs--so save your money!

Vision and Hearing

As with the height/weight requirements, the vision and hearing requirements for major carriers are rigid, and you will be tested prior to employment. It is acceptable to wear contacts and glasses. Once again, if you do not meet these requirements, consider looking into employment with the regional, charter, or commuter carriers.

Additional Minimum Requirements

All the major carriers require a pre-employment physical in which your height/weight, vision, hearing, and general health is tested. This will usually be held at either the airlines medical facility or at a local medical clinic. At this time they will also perform a urine analysis to test for drugs. If you are taking any medication, make sure you let them know. If you do not pass your drug test, you will <u>not</u> be given a second chance. Because flight attendants are in a safety related position, the airline can randomly perform drug and alcohol tests on flight attendants and pilots at any time while on duty - and they will! FAA regulations require that flight attendants and pilots refrain from drinking any alcoholic beverage at least 8 hours prior to duty, and some carriers have an even stricter policy requiring abstinence at least 12 hours prior to duty.

Most major carriers prefer applicants who are fluent in languages in addition to English, the most sought after being Asian languages, Spanish, and French. Also, you must have authorization to work in the United States. If working for an international carrier, you must also have the ability to have multiple exits and entries to the United States.

Most airlines also require that applicants be willing to relocate to any one of their bases. People considering a flight attendant career often ask me about "commuting" from their home town to wherever they may be based. For those of you who are not familiar with commuting, it simply means you do not live in your assigned domicile, and you use your flight privileges to get from your home town to your assigned base. It can be done and many flight attendants do commute successfully. A study done by the Association of Flight Attendants showed that 27% of flight attendants commute by air. If you do plan on commuting, do **not** mention it when you're interviewing. The airlines frown on commuting, due to the risk involved. They're concerned commuting employees will miss their flights to their domiciles and be unable to work their assigned trips. **They want to hear that you are willing to relocate to any domicile you are assigned.**

Desired Traits

We have discussed the bare minimums the airlines have set for flight attendant employment; however, there are obviously many other criteria used to decide which of the thousands of applicants are actually hired. The flight attendant position is one of the most important in the industry, because they have the greatest contact with (and direct influence on) the passenger. A good flight attendant can have a large effect on a passenger's positive flight experience and repeat business. A bad flight attendant, however, can cause an incredible amount if irreparable damage. The list on the following page will give you an idea of what additional traits and training the airlines are looking for.

Personality Traits

- ✈ Friendly
- ✈ Excellent interpersonal skills
- ✈ Dependable
- ✈ Self-disciplined
- ✈ Flexible
- ✈ Good sense of humor
- ✈ Works well under stress
- ✈ Mature
- ✈ Excellent communication skills
- ✈ Considerate
- ✈ Enthusiastic
- ✈ Positive attitude
- ✈ Service oriented
- ✈ Outgoing
- ✈ Intelligent
- ✈ Strong leadership skills
- ✈ High energy level
- ✈ Respect for authority
- ✈ Poise
- ✈ Confidence

This list may represent the "ideal flight attendant", and noone is all of these things all of the time. However, the airlines are looking for people who can handle John Q. Public on a daily basis, and will be looking for applicants who already posses the above traits.

Physical Traits

- ✈ Minimums as noted
- ✈ Clean, fresh appearance
- ✈ Well groomed
- ✈ Good posture
- ✈ Clear skin
- ✈ Clean and manicured fingernails

The myths and stereotypes of "ex-beauty pageant contestant" flight attendants are completely false, which is apparent any time you step into an aircraft. I remember sitting in a group interview and being intimidated by the competition, assuming because they were extremely attractive they were automatically "in". I realized later in training, however, that these individuals were not amongst us - they hadn't made the cut. As I looked at the people around me, it became quite clear that the airlines were hiring well rounded, personable individuals - not Barbie and Ken.

I am not saying your physical appearance will have no effect on the hiring process. The reality is, in this industry, pride in your personal appearance is important. They are seeking individuals who are well groomed and attractive looking, along with possessing likable personalities. They want to hire individuals who will do an excellent job of representing their company. There are enough hopeful candidates that meet these requirements that they aren't going to hire someone that they see as a "project". Make sure you attend your interviews looking polished, showing that you <u>already</u> posses the traits they are looking for. You can find additional information on grooming, and what to wear to the interviews in Chapter 9.

Experience

+ Customer Service
+ Public Contact
+ Food Service
+ Volunteer Work
+ Travel

Once again, the airlines are looking for people who like working with people. Any experience in your past that displays your people skills is a plus. This includes all of the items listed, as well as anything else you can think of. Keep in mind that experience does not need to be paid work to be of value. Be prepared, as these are the kinds of examples of your ability to work with the public you will want to bring up during your interviews.

Training / Skills/ Certification

+ Foreign Language Skills
+ First Aid/CPR Training
+ Military Training
+ Licenses Held
+ Any Additional Training

As noted earlier, the airlines give preference to language qualified candidates. This gives you a big advantage so make sure the airlines are aware of your skill. With some airlines you do not need to be fluent, only conversational. This is not something you want to lie about, as you will usually have to take both an oral and written test. You will receive First Aid/CPR training during the airline's training program; however, it is an added bonus to already have these skills. As previously noted, in the early days all flight attendants had to be nurses. Although it's no longer a requirement, it's still a great benefit to have someone on the aircraft with some additional medical training. Feel free to list any additional training you feel would make you more marketable for this position.

Interests / Honors

+ Extracurricular Activities
+ Sports Teams
+ Clubs / Memberships
+ Fraternities / Sororities
+ Offices Held
+ Honors and Awards

The airlines are looking for individuals who are well rounded. They like to see people who are active and get involved. Be sure to highlight any awards, honors, or achievements you have received, as well as offices held. Note anything that makes you unique, and allows you to stand out from all of the other applicants.

Remember that every time an individual puts on an airline's uniform they are a representative of that particular company. Airlines are going to be looking for individuals that they feel will do an excellent job of representing them on a daily basis. Your job is to convince them that you will do just that, because you have all of the traits that they are looking for in a flight attendant and much more!

What You Can Do Before The Interview To Prepare

✈ **Take care of any appearance problems.**
    - Acne, skin problems - see a Dermatologist
    - Teeth (crooked / stained) - see a Dentist/Orthodontist
    - Hair style/color - see a professional stylist. It's worth spending a little extra money to have your hair professionally colored and styled.
    - Make-up (women)- You can visit the local make-up counter and ask for a complimentary make-over.
    - Nails - Consider a professional manicure.

✈ **Join a gym / health club.**
    This will be great for your physical health, as well as your mental health.

✈ **Learn to swim.**
    Most airlines will test your swimming ability in training. You must demonstrate that you can handle yourself in the unlikely event of an emergency water landing.

✈ **Stop smoking.**
    Some airlines will not hire smokers, and most would prefer not to. All domestic flights are non-smoking, and there is often not enough time for flight attendants to get off the plane between legs. Therefore, chances are you would not be able to smoke during your entire duty period, which may be difficult for someone addicted to nicotine. Also, studies have shown smokers have more health problems than non-smokers, costing the company more money in medical costs and sick days. For these reasons, companies prefer to hire non-smokers and you should try to avoid the problem entirely by attempting to stop before you begin interviewing.

✈ **Know the City Codes and Military Times listed in the Reference section**.
    It's one less thing you'll have to learn in training, and the airlines will be impressed that you took the initiative and time to learn them ahead of time.

✈ **Learn a second language.**
    Most airlines would prefer a candidate who speaks a second language, and some airlines require it. Speaking a foreign language can never hurt, and it may mean the difference between whether you are hired or not. Some airlines consider sign language a second language. Even if you've just begun learning a language and are not yet fluent, the airlines will see that you have taken the initiative and it will be to your benefit.

✈ **Take a CPR class.**
> Once again, you will have CPR/First Aid training once you are accepted for training; however it is an added bonus to already have these skills.

✈ **Do volunteer work.**
> This shows you are a well-rounded, caring individual. It also shows you use your free time productively.

✈ **Learn your geography.**
> Passengers will often ask flight attendants what part of the country they are flying over or to notify them when the aircraft is approaching a certain geographical landmark.

✈ **Get a passport.**
> You will need a passport to fly internationally. Also, some airlines allow their domestic flight attendants with passports to fly internationally when they are short of international flight attendants.

✈ **Practice speaking in front of a group.**
> You can always practice in front of friends and family or join a group such as Toastmasters.

✈ **Read self-help books.**
> Self-help books can help boost your self-esteem and confidence. Pursuing a flight attendant career may take some time, and there may be some rejection involved. Anything that can help you keep a positive mental outlook will be of benefit throughout the challenging hiring process.

Notes

PART II

How To Chose
The Right Employer
For You

Chapter 4

Types Of Carriers

Choosing the right type of employer is extremely important. There has already been a brief reference to the different types of carriers in the previous chapters; however this chapter will explain each type in further detail. Airline carriers can be broken down into four groups of potential employers:

- ✈ **Major**
- ✈ **Regional**
- ✈ **Charter**
- ✈ **Commuter**

In the Airline Directory you will find the names and addresses of the largest employers in each of these categories. Everyone must decide which type of carrier is best for them depending on their individual needs. At this time you must assess why you want to become a flight attendant, which will help to determine the type of airline for which you would be the happiest working. Do you want to fly internationally immediately? Do you want to be home as many nights as possible? Do you want to work for a large, reputable company? A small company? Do you fall short of the minimum qualifications of the major airlines? We will discuss each of the types of airlines in terms of advantages and disadvantages, which should allow you to select the one that best fits your needs.

Major Airlines

To qualify as a major airline, a carrier must generate at least one billion dollars in sales annually. The major carriers only fly jet aircraft, both wide body and narrow body. They also tend to have a very extensive route structure. Examples of **major** carriers would be American, Delta, and United. Major airlines are the largest companies in the industry and therefore offer the most job opportunities, employing approximately 90% of all flight attendants.

Advantages to working for a Major Airline

Flight attendant positions with the major airlines are the most sought after in the industry for several reasons. For one, they tend to offer the strongest incentive packages. Their pay scales, benefits packages, and work conditions tend to be the best in the industry.

Another advantage to working for a major carrier is the diversity in the route structure. The majors have the greatest flight frequency into the largest cities across the U.S., as well as many cities which you've probably never heard of. It's a great way to see America on someone else's tab! Also, many of the major airlines fly internationally, allowing greater opportunities to travel abroad, either while working or while traveling for pleasure.

The major airlines have their bases (or domiciles) in large cities, usually the same locations as their headquarters and hubs. Many are very popular and highly sought after cities in which to live, such as San Francisco, Boston, and Seattle. The chart below lists the major airlines and their respective flight attendant bases.

Company	Flight Attendant Bases
Alaska	Anchorage, Seattle, Long Beach, Portland
American	Dallas, Chicago, Miami, Boston, New York, San Diego, Los Angeles, San Francisco, Washington DC, Nashville, Honolulu, San Juan
America West	Columbus, Los Angeles, Phoenix
Continental	Cleveland, Newark, Houston, Los Angeles
Delta	Atlanta, Boston, Chicago, Cincinnati, Dallas, Houston, Los Angeles, Miami, New Orleans, New York, Orlando, Portland, Salt Lake City, Seattle
Northwest	Minneapolis / St. Paul, Detroit, Memphis, Seattle, New York, Boston, Chicago, Los Angeles, Honolulu, San Francisco
Southwest	Dallas, Houston, Phoenix, Chicago, Oakland
TWA	St. Louis, New York
United	San Francisco, Los Angeles, Seattle, Denver, Chicago, Newark, New York, Philadelphia, Washington DC, Miami, London, Taipei, Paris, Honolulu
US Air	Boston, Philadelphia, Pittsburgh, Los Angeles, Washington DC, Charlotte

Once again, everything is based on seniority. Just because the airline has a base in Honolulu doesn't mean that Waikiki will automatically be your new home. It is often hard to predict if a base is junior or senior, and it can change rapidly if there is a change in a carrier's route structure. When London opened as a base for United, it was very junior and fairly easy to get based there. The senior flight attendants were settled in their lives and had no desire to transfer overseas. As a new hire, you will be placed at the base that needs flight attendants the most. You are usually given a choice between two or three cities; however, this is not always the case. The key is to be flexible, think of it as an adventure, and remember most airlines allow domicile transfers after six months.

There are several other advantages to working for a major carrier, such as the stability and prestige associated with the larger airlines. You can proudly tell everyone you work for "Delta Airlines" and they will be familiar with the company as well as their high quality of service. Because the large companies have been in existence for so many years, there is a level of stability that you would not find with a smaller, start-up company. Although the saying "Nothing is as constant as change" seems as though it was written for the airline industry, the major airlines in general provide more long term stability than other types of carriers.

Disadvantages to working for a Major Airline

Because the major carriers are such large companies, you are given an employee number when you are hired. That is how they will refer to you for the duration of your employment-- as a number. Because of the large volume of flight attendants and the nomadic nature of the position, it is obvious why this type of tracking system is necessary. However, if you are someone who wants to feel as though you are an integral part of a company, this may not be the type of carrier for you. It is also more difficult to maintain long-term friendships with your co-workers, since the majors have thousands of flight attendants flying thousands of different schedules. Just when you meet a crew with which you really bond, you are off to New Jersey and they are off to Los Angeles. It is also more difficult to "move-up" if you have aspirations of pursuing other positions within the company. Because you are just one of thousands, it can be hard to separate yourself among the crowd.

Also, living in a large city is not an ideal situation for everyone. For those who prefer living in a small town, working for a major airline would not be the best option unless you will be commuting. In addition, most of the base cities tend to be fairly expensive places to live, in relation to smaller cities or towns. Flight attendant's beginning salaries can be fairly lean; therefore, communal living is very popular among newly hired flight attendants. Training for a major carrier usually lasts longer than the other types of carriers due to the multiple types of aircraft and more extensive meal/beverage services. The more elaborate in-flight beverage/meal service also can equate to a greater workload on the aircraft, in comparison to other types of airlines.

Regional Airlines

Regional airlines have sales under one billion dollars annually . They fly jet aircraft like the major carriers, but have a more limited route structure. Examples of Regional airlines would be Reno Air, Aloha Airlines, and Frontier Airlines.

Advantages to working for a Regional Airline

There are several advantages to working for a regional carrier. Because the companies tend to be smaller, the flight crews can get to know each another on a more personal basis. It is easier to build stronger friendships and more of a "family" work environment. A smaller work force can also mean less time on reserve and more opportunities to bid for a schedule that meets your requirements, i.e. weekends off, holidays off, etc. A smaller company can also mean greater opportunity for upward mobility, allowing you to become known for your individual abilities and accomplishments.

Regional carriers also offer many of the same advantages that major carriers offer. They tend to still have their bases in fairly large cities, just offering fewer base options than the major carriers. They still fly mainly to the larger cities, which allows for great layovers and pleasure travel, but just have a less extensive route structure.

The regional carriers often offer a more limited in-flight service, meaning reduced in-flight requirements for the flight attendants. Also, the regional carriers tend to fly only one or two types of aircraft, making the training period for flight attendants much shorter. If you did not meet the minimum requirements for the major carriers in terms of age, height/weight, and vision, you might want to consider working for a regional carrier.

Disadvantages to working for a Regional Airline

When you compare working for a regional carrier to a major carrier, there are several disadvantages. As stated earlier, the benefit packages for regional carriers are usually not as strong. For the regional carriers that do not have union representation, the work conditions can be more demanding, requiring longer duty periods and fewer days off. Also, because the major carriers have been in service for so many years, they tend to offer greater long term stability than the regional carriers. This also affects the degree of prestige associated with regional carriers, as many people are unfamiliar with the carriers due to their limited flight service. Since the regional carriers have a more condensed route structure, you are limited to the locations that you can travel on your carrier for free, although most other carriers offer excellent discounts to other airline employees.

Charter Airlines

Charter airlines cater to tour groups, rock bands, sports teams, etc. They usually do not sell tickets to the general public. The routes they fly vary depending on the needs of the individual group with which they have contracted. Most charters operate jet aircraft, both narrow body and wide body.

Advantages to working for a Charter Airline

There are several advantages to working for a charter airline. The first of which is the variety of places the charters service. With most of the major airlines, it may be years before you have the required seniority to fly internationally. With a charter you may have the opportunity to go to Paris on your first trip. Most of the places charters service are vacation and tourist spots, so it's a great job to see some of the most exotic and interesting places in the world. Much like the regional carriers, the charter airlines tend to be smaller. It's easier for the crews to become a close knit group because they often remain with the tour group. If the tour group is spending a week in Cancun, then so is the crew! You also have an opportunity to meet some extremely interesting passengers, as charters cover professional sports teams, performance groups, etc. Like the regional carriers, you may not have to be on reserve as long due to the smaller work force. And once again, if you do not meet the minimum requirements for the major airlines, you might want to consider pursuing a career with the charter companies.

Disadvantages to working for a Charter Airline

Just as there are unique advantages in working for a charter airline, there are also unique disadvantages. There are examples of charters that have very sound reputations and long term stability, such as American Trans Air. In general, however, the charter carriers tend to be the least stable of the different types of carriers. When analyzing the airlines that have started-up and folded over the last ten years, many were charters. Furloughs are also a threat, as a charter may have several tours booked through a season, but then may have a slump in business. Furloughs consist of the airlines reducing their work force when demand slows down and they no longer need all of their employees on the payroll. You are not fired, and if the need arises for your position, you will be given an opportunity to return before someone else can be hired for your job. Also, someone who is married with children at home may not have the same excitement about spending two weeks in Paris as a single person who has never traveled abroad. And as with some regional carriers, the duty periods for charters may be longer and more demanding.

Commuter Airlines

Commuter airlines offer service to smaller cities in propeller driven aircraft. The prop planes seat 15-75 passengers and usually do not fly trips much longer than one hour. They tend to be smaller companies and are often based in smaller cities. Most (although not all) commuter airlines are affiliated with a major airline. They offer service to the smaller cities that the majors do not. The chart on the following page lists the major airlines and the larger of the commuter airlines with which they are affiliated. You will find all of these carriers listed in the Airline Directory located in the Reference section of this guide.

Major Airline	Commuter Affiliate
American	American Eagle / Flagship Airlines
Continental	Continental Express
Delta	Delta Connection / Atlantic Southeast Airlines Delta Connection / Business Express Delta Connection / Skywest Airlines
Trans World Airlines	Trans States Trans World Express
United	United Express / Air Wisconsin United Express / Atlantic Coast Airlines United Express / Great Lakes Airlines United Express / Mesa Airlines United Express / Mesaba
US Air	US Air Express / CC Air US Air Express / Allegheny Commuter Airlines US Air Express / Piedmont US Air Express / PSA

Advantages to working for a Commuter Airline

Working for a commuter airline has several advantages. As discussed earlier, the commuter carriers tend to be smaller, allowing more interaction with the crews as well as additional opportunities for upward mobility within the company. Because of the smaller work force, much like the charter and regional carriers, you may not have to be on reserve as long, allowing you more freedom with your schedule. Also, due to the small aircraft, you will have an opportunity to really interact with the passengers rather than just bark "chicken or beef" in their general direction.

For those who do not want to live in a big city, this may be the type of carrier for you. Most commuter carriers are located in smaller cities and therefore have their bases in smaller cities. Also, if you want to sleep in your own bed every night, the commuter airlines are your best bet. Because they fly shorter legs, many have their flight attendants home almost every night. And due to the limited space on the aircraft and short flying times, most commuters only offer a beverage service. This again reduces the flight attendant's work load on the aircraft, as well as reducing the length of training time. In addition, you may be the only flight attendant on the aircraft, which many flight attendants enjoy.

Because the commuter airlines are often affiliated with major airlines, some flight attendants will work for a commuter airline to test whether it's a job they really enjoy. If they want to continue a career as a flight attendant, they will then try to get hired by the affiliated major carrier. And once again, for those who do not fit within the major carriers guidelines, the commuter airlines tend to be more lenient. As stated earlier, some commuter airlines actually prefer shorter candidates, simply for the ease with which they can move through the smaller aircraft.

Disadvantages to working for a Commuter Airline

As the pay scale on the following page indicates, the commuter airlines tend to have the lowest compensation plan of all the carriers. The job can also be the most difficult due to the conditions that occur in prop planes versus jets. The planes are smaller and must fly at a lower altitude, which can result in a much bumpier ride. Also, due to the limited routes and the type of cities they service, you would be more likely to have a layover in Paris, Texas, than Paris, France. Working for a commuter airline can be demanding since the legs are shorter and there are more of them. Instead of working three legs in a day, you might work five or six. And for those people looking for a choice of several large cities for bases, this would probably not be the best option for you.

Benefits / Pay Scales

Most of the airlines provide medical/dental benefits, as well as retirement options. As noted previously, the major carriers tend to have the best overall benefits package. The charts below give examples of beginning first year flight attendant salaries.

What You Can Expect For A First Year Starting Salary

Carriers	Average Pay / Month *	Hourly Rate Above Guarantee
Major	$1,000-$1,600	$14.00-$20.00
Regional	$ 900-$1,200	$13.00-$17.00
Charter	$1,000-$1,200	$13.00-$17.00
Commuter	$ 850-$1,100	$11.00-$15.00

* These amounts are based on a monthly guarantee of 65-75 flight hours per month

Major Airlines Starting Salaries

CARRIERS	PAY SCALE
ALASKA	$13.37 / TRIP OR 243 AIR MILES
AMERICA WEST	$12,852 / YEAR
AMERICAN	$16.07/FLIGHT HOUR W/ GUAR. MIN. OF 67 HRS.
CONTINENTAL	$15.00/FLIGHT HOUR W/ GUAR. MIN. OF 83 HRS.
DELTA	$1300/MONTH FOR GUAR. OF 50 HRS.
NORTHWEST	$941.20/MONTH FOR GUAR. OF 65 HRS. - $14.48/HR
SOUTHWEST	$13.60 / 243 AIR MILES
TWA	$942.00/MONTH FOR GUAR. OF 65 HRS. - $14.49/HR.
UNITED	$19.01/FLIGHT HOUR W/ GUAR. MIN OF 65 HRS.
US AIR	$14.61/FLIGHT HOUR W/ GUAR. MIN. OF 65 HRS.

Some airlines pay by the air miles, however most pay by the flight hour, or "block to block", which is explained below. Some are on a standard forty hour/week schedule and pay a regular hourly rate. With all the carriers, flight attendants start off making the same amount of money, regardless of their past experience or educational background. They also receive the same incremental pay increases based strictly on length of service, not on performance.

Compensation Plan For Flight Attendants

In the "flight attendant world" you are usually paid by the amount of flight hours or block time you accumulate. This is measured by the time the aircraft pushes away from the gate at its point of departure, until the time the aircraft is parked at the gate at its point of arrival. Most airlines guarantee a flight attendant from 65-75 flight hours per month, which is the amount shown under the heading "average pay/month" on the previous chart. If you are on reserve and do not fly your minimum number of hours, you will still get paid the minimum guaranteed amount.

Some airlines limit the number of hours a flight attendant can work per month, however other airlines have no maximum. This is where the "hourly wage above guarantee" column comes in. Any hours above your minimum guarantee worked will be paid at the hourly rate. As an example:

Francine flight attendant has a guarantee of $1200.00/month for 75 flight hours. Her hourly rate above her guarantee is $17.00 and she worked 90 flight hours this month. She will earn her $1200.00, plus $255.00 (15 hours x $17.00) or $1455.00.

All airline carriers also provide per diem (literally "per day"), which is money allocated for meal expenses while on a trip. It ranges from $1.00-$2.00/hour and is paid from the time you check-in for a trip until the time you arrive back at your base and check-out. Example; If you were on a trip for 48 hours and received $2.00/hour in per diem, your per diem allowance for that 2-day trip would be $96.00. Most flight attendants earn an additional $350.00-$500.00 per month in per diem (even more if they are flying internationally). There is also additional pay of $1.00-$2.00/flight hour for working positions that require additional paperwork and responsibility. Most carriers also offer incremental pay for working holidays, overtime, and flying internationally.

Unions

When choosing an employer you will also want to find out if the flight attendants are members of a union. I started my flight attendant job search as a recent college graduate with a business degree. After studying management, I had personal beliefs that unions had their time and place and were no longer necessary. My opinion on the subject changed after working for an airline that was unionized and one that was not. The working conditions, pay scales, and benefits are (in general) better for unionized carriers than for non-union airlines. Of the major airlines, only Delta Airlines in non-union.

If you are a member of a union, you will be responsible for monthly union dues of approximately $30.00. For this fee the union ensures the flight attendants are getting the strongest compensation, benefit, and work rules package possible, as well as legal representation. It can have a significant impact on your job responsibilities as well as your financial future, so it is definitely something you will want to consider when pursuing a flight attendant position.

I am not saying all carriers without a flight attendant union offer poor work conditions. Keep in mind these are generalities. Some airlines treat their employees fairly, and therefore a union is not necessary. One of the best ways to get a feel for how a company treats their employees, union or no union, is to talk to the employees themselves. Try to speak to several individuals in a variety of different positions, to get a realistic feel of how enjoyable the work environment really is.

Hopefully you have a better feel for the different types of carriers and what each has to offer. The statements concerning each of the carriers are obviously generalities, opinions, or general reputations, and will not be true for every carrier within that category. It is important to assess your needs and focus in on the type (or types) of carriers for which you would most like to work and begin your job search from there. There is a suitable employer for everyone; it's just deciding what it is you want out of your career as a flight attendant. Once you have made a decision on the right type of carrier for you, move on to the next chapter where you will discover how to tackle the application process.

Notes

Notes

PART III

How To Present Yourself In The Most Impressive Way Throughout The Application Process

Chapter 5
General Guidelines

It's time to begin the application process. There are several ways to discover which airlines are currently hiring flight attendants. The best method is to check your local Sunday paper in the Help Wanted section under "Airline" or "Flight Attendant". Most major carriers will place ads one to two weeks prior to their interview date, otherwise referred to as an Open House. These interviews are also called "cattle calls" since some of the larger carriers will have thousands of applicants respond. The interviews are normally held at local hotels, and applicants are handled on a first come first serve basis.

They usually have several sessions available throughout the day, such as 9:00 AM, 12:00 PM, and 3:00 PM, and it is definitely to your advantage to be one of the first to arrive. I have known several people who were unable to interview because they arrived for the last session, and were bumped by applicants who could not be accommodated from earlier sessions. By attending one of these "cattle calls" you can eliminate a great deal of time in the interviewing process, as it's an indication that the airlines are looking to hire flight attendants **immediately**. In Chapter 10 you will learn what to expect from this type of interview, as well as how to master it.

The next method would be to utilize the job hot line numbers listed in the Airline Directory located in the Reference section. These numbers give extremely useful information, such as the positions the airlines are currently hiring for, what qualifications they are seeking in an applicant, and specific instructions on how to apply. The information on the hot line numbers is usually updated frequently, so this is a great way to have access to the most current hiring information.

The next option is to make a trip to your closest airport and visit the airline ticket counters. Some airlines distribute applications this way, (Southwest, Delta) however not all of them do. It will depend upon the individual carriers' policy, as well as the amount of service that airline provides at that particular airport.

If the company for which you are interested in working has not advertised, does not have a job hot line number, or the job hot line number states they are not currently hiring flight attendants, do not get discouraged. The airline industry changes quickly. A company that has not hired in years may acquire additional routes and suddenly be looking to hire hundreds of flight attendants immediately. It will pay to be one step ahead of the competition, so you should begin the application process right away. If they airline does begin hiring, they will give preference to the applications and resumes they already have on file. Sometimes they will only grant Open House interviews to individuals who already have their application or resume on file.

Unless specified otherwise by the job hot line #, you should adhere to the following steps when applying for a flight attendant position. Always send an "employment packet" to prospective employers. This includes a personalized "requesting an application" cover letter (see example in Chapter 6), resume (see example in Chapter 7), and self - addressed stamped envelope with $.64 postage affixed. The self-addressed stamped envelope is for the airline to send an application and any additional information they have on the position. Most companies will specifically request a self-addressed stamped envelope, but for those that do not, it may speed up the time it will take to receive your application. All of this should be packaged in a large "9x12" envelope. This will keep your resume and cover letter from getting folded, as well as setting you apart from the thousands of other applicants. Some airlines may actually return your resume with the application they send you, which just means that particular carrier does not retain resumes on file. The qualifications of a good cover letter, resume, and application will be covered n the following chapters.

When beginning your flight attendant search, it is imperative you remain organized. You must be on top of your correspondence with prospective employers at all times. In the Reference section you will find a "Job Log", which can be used to help track your communication with the respective airlines. You should also maintain a file on each carrier for which you are interested in working, keeping copies of every piece of information either sent to or received from them. It will be extremely helpful to have this information for review prior to an interview. They will also have a file on you, in which they keep copies of everything you have sent to them.

Keep in mind that whatever you send to a carrier is a written representation of yourself. Until you get your foot in the door for a personal interview, your written correspondence is the only way the airlines will be able to judge you. It is imperative that everything they receive from you is organized, neat, and grammatically correct. You want to present yourself as professionally as possible. Remember that airlines are looking for ways to eliminate people, and this is a very easy one.

Some airlines will respond immediately, while others will take weeks to respond. Just be patient and realize they are inundated with thousands of employment requests. If you have not heard anything in 6-8 weeks, submit another resume and "no response" cover letter (see example in Chapter 6) stating your continued interest. It can't hurt for them to see your name across their desk more than once, and your persistence will represent your deep desire to work for their company.

Once again, it is important to record all correspondence in your "Job Log" for future reference. You may receive an application, you may receive a letter stating they are not currently hiring but will keep your resume on file, or you may be contacted for an interview. The following chapters will discuss how to handle each one of these situations.

So just as a review, here are the steps you should follow:

- ✈ Check the local Sunday paper for airlines interviewing in your area.
- ✈ Call the job hot line #'s of the carriers you are interested in working for and follow instructions on how to apply (if given).
- ✈ Go to your nearest airport and visit the ticket counters of the airlines for which you are interested in working.
- ✈ If not given specific application instructions by the job hot line #'s, send an "employment packet" to the companies you are interested in.
- ✈ Record everything in your Job Log.

The next three chapters will cover the resume, cover letter, and completion of the application. Continue on to learn what the airlines will be looking for concerning each of these areas, and how to avoid making costly mistakes that could get you eliminated from the interviewing process.

Notes

Chapter 6

The Cover Letter

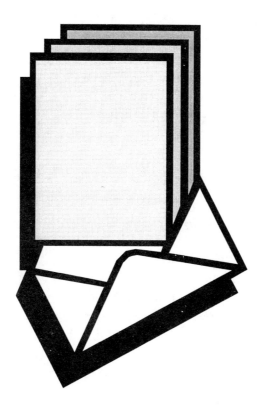

The cover letter is extremely important because once again, it is one of the first pieces of correspondence you will have with your prospective employer. When your letter is neat, clear, and well organized, they will have the same impression of <u>you</u>. A cover letter should be sent when 1)you are requesting an application 2) with a completed application 3) when you have not received a response and 4) as a thank-you letter after receiving an interview. There are examples of each of these types of cover letters on the following pages. Listed below are some guidelines for an effective cover letter:

✈ Use a high quality paper, medium to heavy weight, preferably white or off-white.

✈ Make sure there are no errors in spelling, punctuation, or grammar.

✈ Try to address it to a particular person, rather than just to "Personnel" (unless instructed otherwise). Utilize the Airline Directory to call the airline's headquarters and get a contact name. Ask for the name of the person in charge of hiring flight attendants. Some will give you the information (usually the smaller carriers), and some will not. If you are able to get a name, remember to note it in your "Job Log". Always have the name spelled out for you.

✈ Always enclose a copy of your resume, unless specifically told not to.

✈ Use a typewriter or word processor to create your letters. If using a word processor, print on a letter quality or laser printer.

✈ Keep your letters to one page, with good use of the white space. Use your words wisely, using short, concise sentences.

✈ Tailor your skills and qualifications to the flight attendant position.

✈ Send all correspondence promptly. Thank-you letters should be mailed out within 24 hours of your interview.

✈ Thank-you letters should be sent after each interview you receive, which not only shows proper etiquette, but will leave a positive impression with the interviewer (I had a boss who said he wouldn't anyone unless they sent a thank-you note after an interview, no matter how much he liked them or how qualified they were!) It's a small gesture that can go a long way. This is also a great opportunity to add anything you forgot to mention in the interview or to reiterate your strengths and achievements.

✈ Always use Mr./Ms./Mrs. in your correspondence.

✈ Make sure you have enough postage on all correspondence.

✈ Allow your unique personality to shine through. There are definitely specific guidelines you must follow; however, they do not want to see a generic cover letter. Detail the achievements that not only qualify you for the job, but that make you a unique individual.

On the following pages you will find sample cover letters. Do not "copy" these letters, but instead use them as a guideline for the basic information your letters should contain.

Cover Letter Outline

Your Address
Your City, State, Zip Code

Today's Date

Recipient's Name
Position
Company
Address
City, State, Zip Code

Greeting/Salutation: (Dear Mr./Ms./Mrs.)

    1st Paragraph - State the Purpose/Objective/Position Desired

    2nd Paragraph- Highlight Your Skills/Qualifications Relevant to the Flight
        Attendant Position

    3rd Paragraph - Close/Ask for Action

        Sincerely,

        Your Signature

        Your Name Printed

Sample Cover Letter
Requesting An Application

222 Maple Lane
Anywhere, CA 94000

May 5, 1995

Jane Doe
Director of In-flight
ABC Airlines
San Francisco Int'l Airport
San Francisco, CA 94536

Dear Ms. Doe:

I am seeking a career as a flight attendant with ABC Airlines, and feel with my qualifications I could be a strong asset to your company.

I am a recent graduate of San Francisco State University, with a BS in Business Administration and a minor in French. While attending school, I received extensive customer service training as a sales representative for a women's clothing store. With my educational training, fluency in French, and excellent human relations skills, I feel I could be a positive addition to ABC Airlines.

I am very enthusiastic about beginning a career as a flight attendant for ABC Airlines, and would appreciate it if you could send me an employment application at your earliest convenience.

Sincerely,

Iwanna Fly

Sample Cover Letter
No Response To An Application Request

222 Maple Lane
Anywhere, CA 94000

May 5, 1995

Jane Doe
Director of In-flight
ABC Airlines
San Francisco Int'l Airport
San Francisco, CA 94536

Dear Ms. Doe:

I sent a letter requesting a flight attendant application on March 10th, and have not yet received one. I am still extremely interested in obtaining a flight attendant position with ABC Airlines, and would appreciate it if you could send me an application at your earliest convenience.

With my educational training , fluency in French, extensive experience working with the general public, and strong desire to continue in a customer service related career, I feel I could be a strong asset to ABC Airlines.

Thank you in advance for your attention to this matter.

Sincerely,

Iwanna Fly

Sample Cover Letter
With Completed Application

222 Maple Lane
Anywhere, CA 94000

May 5, 1995

Jane Doe
Director of In-flight
ABC Airlines
San Francisco Int'l Airport
San Francisco, CA 94536

Dear Ms. Doe:

I am returning my completed flight attendant application. I have also enclosed a resume, which offers additional information concerning my educational training, work history and personal achievements.

As a student putting myself through college, I had the opportunity to work as sales representative in a women's clothing store for several years. This position not only allowed me to work with the general public on a daily basis, but was an excellent opportunity to enhance my human relation and customer service skills. With my educational training , fluency in French, and strong desire to continue in a customer service related career, I feel I could be a strong asset to ABC Airlines.

I look forward to meeting you in person to discuss my qualifications in greater detail.

Sincerely,

Iwanna Fly

Sample Cover Letter
Thank-you

222 Maple Lane
Anywhere, CA 94000

May 5, 1995

Jane Doe
Director of In-flight
ABC Airlines
San Francisco, CA 94536

Dear Ms. Doe:

I interviewed for a flight attendant position on Thursday, April 13. I wanted to thank you for taking time to discuss possible career opportunities with ABC Airlines.

I am very enthusiastic about a flight attendant position with ABC Airlines. With my extensive customer service experience, fluency in French, and strong desire to continue working with the general public, I feel I have a great deal to contribute to your company.

If you have any additional questions or are in need of additional information, please contact me at (415) 444-4444. I look forward to hearing from you soon.

Sincerely,

Iwanna Fly

Notes

Chapter 7

The Resume

Creating a resume can be extremely challenging, when you consider you're being asked to summarize your entire life's history on one page. Because the airlines receive so many resumes, they can only spend a limited time reviewing each one. Statistics show that your resume will probably get 30 seconds of an interviewer's attention **at the most**, and 10-15 seconds is probably more accurate. To add to the challenge, the airlines receive so many resumes they are constantly looking for ways to eliminate applicants. You must create a resume that gives a clear, concise picture of who you are, what you have accomplished, and why you would be an excellent addition to their company.

There are several options available when preparing a resume. You can utilize a professional resume service, or you can create one yourself. One advantage to creating it yourself, is that only **you** know your own individual strengths and achievements; therefore, you are the best one to reveal those talents.

Another advantage to preparing your own resume is that it forces you to really analyze and review your skills and achievements, prior to the interviewing process. Only when you have a good handle on your personal experiences, skills, and accomplishments, can you give your strongest sales pitch to the airlines as to why they should hire **you** above all the other applicants.

On the following pages you will find resume worksheets to help you prepare your own "individual" resume. It will require some additional work on your part, however the effort will pay off. The end result will be an original selling tool that highlights exactly why you are the strongest candidate for the job.

Resume Worksheet

Employment History
Start with the most recent

Employer_____

Title held_____

Dates Employed_____ to _____

Responsibilities & Duties_____

Accomplishments & Results_____

_____

_____

Employer_____

Title Held_____

Dates Employed_____ to _____

Responsibilities & Duties_____

_____

_____

Accomplishments & Results_____

_____

_____

Employer_____

Title Held_____

Dates Employed_____ to _____

Responsibilities & Duties_____

_____

_____

Accomplishments & Results_____

_____

_____

Additional Experience

(Example; volunteer work, church activities, social service, military experience, travel, living abroad, etc.)

_____
_____
_____
_____
_____

Additional Skills / Training / Certification

(Example; foreign language skills, special seminars, first aid/CPR training, cosmetology licensee, travel agent certification)

_____
_____
_____
_____
_____

Interests

(Example; teams, memberships, clubs, associations, sororities/fraternities, extracurricular activities, hobbies)

_____
_____
_____
_____
_____

Honors

(Example; awards, offices held, titles)

_____
_____
_____
_____
_____

Educational History

Start with the most recent. If you went to three different colleges, just note the school from which you graduated or last attended. The same applies for high schools.

School Name_____
City and State_____
Dates Attended_____to_____
Courses Studied_____
Degree Received_____
Grade Point Average (Show the scale example; 3.5/4.0)_____

School Name_____
City and State_____
Dates Attended_____to_____
Courses Studied_____
Degree Received_____
Grade Point Average (Show the scale example; 3.5/4.0)_____

School Name_____
City and State_____
Dates Attended_____to_____
Courses Studied_____
Degree Received_____
Grade Point Average (Show the scale example; 3.5/4.0)_____

Do's & Don'ts

Before you begin to put your resume together, here are a list of Do's and Don'ts that will help you to create a winning resume.

Do keep your resume to one page, definitely not more than two. This can be achieved by keeping it concise, using short sentences, and avoiding repetition.

Do use a high quality paper, medium to heavy weight, either white or off-white color.

Do check for errors in grammar, spelling, or punctuation.

Do make it is easy to read (neat, clean, well organized). Use bullets to organize and enhance readability. Leave at least a 1" border all around and utilize the white space. You don't want to group too much text together.

Do emphasize results, achievements, and accomplishments more than responsibilities and duties.

Do begin statements with action verbs (see the list of action verbs on page 54)

Do remember, if using a word processor, to use a typeset of 10 pt or greater, a letter quality printer (laser or ink jet), only black ink, and a conservative typeface. Otherwise, have it professionally typeset.

Do continue to edit until you are completely satisfied with your results.

Do have at least two people proofread it for you.

Do be completely accurate (never lie!).

Do tailor your resume to the flight attendant position. Stress previous experience that is similar to the flight attendant requirements and desired traits listed in Chapter 3.

Do include a phone number where you can be reached, or have an answering machine with a professional message.

Do include your grades only if they are strong (3.0 or better on 4.0 scale).

Don't state your age, gender, weight, marital status, origin, race, religion, or political affiliation.

Don't enclose a picture, unless specifically asked to.

Don't use I, me, or my.

Don't write "RESUME" at the top of your resume (they'll figure it out!)

Don't use all capitals.

Don't abbreviate (except for dates i.e. 3/95)

Don't go nuts on the boldface, italic print, or underlining. Save those for special emphasis.

Don't include references. You can present those on request.

Don't try to be funny. Your resume isn't the place to practice a new stand-up comedy routine.

Don't make corrections to your resume in pen, crayon, etc. If your resume needs to be updated, you must create a new resume.

Don't state a requested salary. Flight attendant salaries are not negotiable. Everyone is paid the same regardless of their experience or educational training.

Don't try to use tricks or gimmicks to get your resume noticed (i.e. fluorescent paper).

Don't use the resume to state reasons for leaving previous employers (layoffs, firings, etc.).

Additional Tips On Preparing A Winning Resume

➔ List only your most recent jobs. If you have additional jobs from your past that you feel are relevant to the flight attendant position, you can group them together. Example; 1975-1980 Extensive experience working with the public in the food service industry

➔ If you are a recent college graduate, you will probably want to put your education before your experience. If you have extensive experience and have been out of school for some time, you probably want to put your experience first.

novel

Action Verbs To Enhance Your Resume

Achieved	Accomplished	Analyzed
Appointed	Arranged	Attained
Budgeted	Calculated	Certified
Communicated	Compiled	Completed
Conducted	Constructed	Consulted
Controlled	Convinced	Counseled
Created	Decided	Delivered
Demonstrated	Designed	Determined
Developed	Directed	Discovered
Eliminated	Encouraged	Established
Evaluated	Executed	Exhibited
Facilitated	Formulated	Founded
Generated	Handled	Headed
Implemented	Improved	Increased
Initiated	Instituted	Instructed
Introduced	Led	Maintained
Managed	Marketed	Monitored
Motivated	Negotiated	Obtained
Operated	Organized	Oversaw
Participated	Performed	Planned
Presented	Produced	Promoted
Projected	Published	Persuaded
Recommended	Recruited	Reduced
Reported	Represented	Researched
Resolved	Revised	Selected
Served	Sold	Solved
Specified	Strengthened	Summarized
Supervised	Supported	Tested
Trained	Traveled	Uncovered
Undertook	Utilized	Verified
Won	Worked	Wrote

Sample Resume Layout

Full Name (with middle initial)
Complete Address (do not abbreviate)
City, State, Zip Code (do not abbreviate)
Area Code and Phone Number (number where you can be reached at all times)

Specific Objective: Example; To begin a challenging career as a flight
                           attendant with a major airline carrier.

Experience: most recent   Company
                                 City & State
                                 Dates of employment
                                 Results/Achievements/Duties/Responsibilities
                                 Promotions, Honors

next most recent
next most recent

Education: College: Name of School
                             Type of degree you received
                             Dates Attended

High school (If no college):   Name of School
                               Dates Attended
                               Special training or courses studied

Additional Training: Languages spoken other than English
                            First aid training / CPR
                            Military training
                            Licenses held

Memberships, Honors, Awards: Club involvement
                                    Offices held
                                    Volunteer work
                                    Special honors received

Activities and Interests: Sports teams
                                 Hobbies
                                 Unique interests

Notes

Chapter 8

The Application

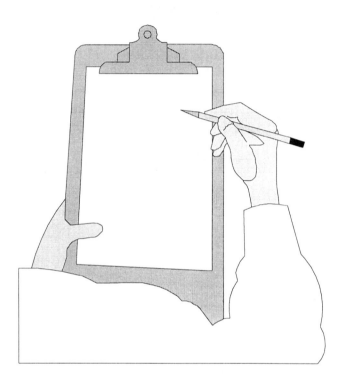

"How hard can filling out an application be?" you ask. Well, believe it or not, this is how a great deal of applicants get themselves eliminated immediately from the hiring process. Some airlines actually score applications, and choose those who qualify for an interview based on this score. Although not all the carriers use a scoring system, all are "grading" your application on neatness, completeness, accuracy, ability to follow instruction, and content.

Once you receive an application, the first thing you should do is make a copy of it. This allows you to make mistakes on the copy and not the original. All applications will require the same basic information so a sample application has been provided for you. Once it is completed, it will eliminate the need to gather the information each time you receive an additional application. Much of this information you can retrieve from your resume worksheet. It will also be to your advantage to have a copy of the completed sample application with you during the interviewing process, as they often require you to fill out an application on the spot, and you will have all the necessary information in front of you.

Sample Application

Personal Information

Name- Last _____ First _____ Middle _____

Social Security Number _____ Today's Date _____

Present Address _____ City _____ State _____ Zip _____ How Long? _____

Permanent Address _____ City _____ State _____ Zip _____ How Long? _____

Home Telephone Number _____ Alternate Number _____

Are you at least 18 years of age? _____

Are you a U.S. Citizen or legally eligible to work in the United States? _____

If you are not a citizen, provide an alien registration number or other authorization number _____

Are you willing to relocate? _____ If "yes", any restrictions _____ Base Preferred _____

Salary requirements _____ How soon would you be available for employment? _____

Are you willing to work nights, holidays, weekends, and irregular hours? _____ If "no", explain _____
_____

Have you previously interviewed for this position with this company? _____ If "yes" date and location _____
_____

State name and job title of relatives employed by this airline and their relationship to you _____
_____

Have you ever been employed with any airline? _____ If "yes", name of airline, job title, and dates _____
_____

Have you ever been convicted of driving under the influence (DUI) or driving while intoxicated within the last 7 years? _____ "If "yes" explain fully _____

Have you been convicted of a misdemeanor within the past 7 years, other than traffic violations? _____
If "yes" explain fully _____

Have you ever been convicted of a felony? _____ If "yes", explain fully _____
_____

Work Experience

List a complete history of all employers (including part-time and temporary employment) for the past ten years.

Previous or Last Employer_____
Address_____
City, State, Zip_____
Phone Number_____
Dates of Employment _____to_____
Supervisors Name and Title_____
Beginning Salary_____Ending Salary_____
Job Title and Duties_____
Reason for Leaving_____

Previous or Last Employer_____
Address_____
City, State, Zip_____
Phone Number_____
Dates of Employment _____to_____
Supervisors Name and Title_____
Beginning Salary_____Ending Salary_____
Job Title and Duties_____
Reason for Leaving_____

Previous or Last Employer_____
Address_____
City, State, Zip_____
Phone Number_____
Dates of Employment _____to_____
Supervisors Name and Title_____
Beginning Salary_____Ending Salary_____
Job Title and Duties_____
Reason for Leaving_____

Attach an additional sheet if necessary.

Periods of Unemployment: In the space below account for all time in excess of 30 days during the last five years when you were not employed, in school, or in the U.S. Military Service.

Dates	Activity (Seeking work, Travel ,etc.)	Name of reference who can confirm (non-relative)	Telephone number

Previous job you enjoyed the most and why_____
_____

Previous job you enjoyed the least and why_____
_____

Will you receive a satisfactory reference from your current and all previous employers? If "no", explain_____
_____

Have you ever been suspended, discharged, or asked to resign by an employer? If so, whom, when, and why?_____
_____

On how many occasions (not days) were you absent from school or work during the last 12 months? (exclude vacations)_____
How many total days of absence did this represent_____
How many times were you late for school or work in the last 12 months_____

Military Experience

Date Entered	Date Discharged	Branch of Service	Rank when entered	Rank end of service or current rank

Positions held and nature of duties_____
_____

Did you receive a dishonorable discharge? If "yes", explain fully_____
_____
_____

Education

Type	Name of School	Location	Courses / Degree	Dates	Did you graduate?
High School / GED					
College					
Vocational					
Other					

Give reason if you attended but did not complete college or trade school_____

_____

Extracurricular activities - high school and college_____

_____

Membership in civic, social or professional organizations which have provided you job related skills_____

_____

Interests and Hobbies_____

_____

Special Awards or Honors (include dates)_____

_____

Language Skills

LANGUAGE	NATIVE	EXCELLENT	CONVERSATIONAL	LIMITED
_____	☐	☐	☐	☐
_____	☐	☐	☐	☐
_____	☐	☐	☐	☐

Physical Data

Do you wear contacts or glasses?_____

Uncorrected vision if you wear contacts or glasses   L_____   R_____

Corrected vision if you wear contacts or glasses   L_____   R_____

Height_____   Weight_____

Heaviest weight in the last 12 mo._____   Lightest weight in the last 12 mo._____

Personal References

Name	Occupation	Address / Phone #

In addition, some applications may ask questions such as:
- "Why do you want to work for this company?"
- "What do you consider your most outstanding personal qualities or characteristics ?"
- "If hired, what personal adjustments in your life would you expect to be necessary ?"

To get hints on how to answer these questions, please review Chapter 11 titled "The Most Commonly Asked Interview Questions" in the following section.

Once you have made a copy of the airline application, read through it entirely before filling it out. Make sure you have all the information you will need to complete it and follow the instructions carefully. Some applications require the applicant to print their name in the space indicated vertically along the side of the first page. This is an opportunity for the airlines to test an applicant's thoroughness and ability to follow directions, so don't forget to fill out this section.

Complete the copy as you would the original. **Never** leave a space blank. If something does not apply to you, simply write N/A (not applicable) in the space. Make sure all your names, dates and phone numbers are completely accurate. Because you are applying for a safety related position, all the airlines are required by law to do an extremely thorough background check. They will check your history a minimum of five years back. If you list someone as a reference or previous employer, rest assured they will be contacted. It's always a good idea to ask someone's permission prior to using them as a reference, as well as asking them what they will say. You may find they're not as great a reference as you thought, but at least you will know before any damage has been done. Keep in mind you are filling out a legal document and all the information must be completely accurate. I knew a fellow flight attendant who had been with the company for a year when they found out she had lied on her application. She was terminated immediately and had no legal recourse. Do not take any chances -- take the time and do it right the first time.

Additional Tips On Filling Out The Application

✈   When asked whether you have filled out an application with that particular carrier before, be honest. They are only asking for their records, so that they don't have two files on "Jim Smith."

✈   When asked about relocation and base preferences, remember they are looking for people who are willing to relocate anywhere.

✈   When asked if you are willing to work nights, holidays, weekends, irregular hours, remember once again, they want to hire people who are extremely flexible. The only acceptable answer is yes.

✈   When asked about availability or a start date, you can state "immediately" if you are not currently employed. If you are currently employed, state two weeks from notification, giving your employer the necessary time to find a replacement for you.

✈   When asked your reason for leaving a position, try to keep it positive. Examples of positive responses would be "to pursue a more challenging position" or "career advancement". Do not state "Because my boss was a tyrant!"

✈   Once again, be completely accurate with all dates of employment, education, and references. Never lie!

✈   When asked about previous job duties and responsibilities in the Employment History section, relate your experience to the flight attendant position. Remember the traits they are seeking, as noted in Chapter 3.

✈   They don't like to see large gaps in employment (over 30 days). Some acceptable reasons for a gap would be school, travel, volunteer work. Some reasons that may send up a red flag would be personal illness / injury or "no reason" (may appear to be a bit lazy).

✈   If asked about salary, simply state "open". The airlines do not negotiate salaries. Everyone begins at the same rate of pay, regardless of their experience or education.

✈   Remember to sign and date the application.

If you feel your rough draft is complete and accurate, you may start to fill out the original application. If you have **very** legible handwriting, you may fill out the application by printing. If not, it should be typed (which is what I recommend anyway). Some airlines actually state that the application must be typed, so carefully read the fine print. You should have someone proof read it to check for typing and grammatical errors. Try to have the application completed and sent within 24-48 hours of receipt. As stated earlier, airlines receive thousands of applications a day and seniority is everything. The sooner you get your application in the mail, the sooner you'll be on your way to a career as a flight attendant. When I was hired by United, they were in the beginning of a major hiring spree. Had I waited just 6 months longer to begin training, there would have been over 1,000 flight attendants senior to me, rather than the other way around. Do not procrastinate -- you will pay for it later!

Remember to make a copy of your application for your files prior to submission. Most major carriers require an application processing fee ranging from $15.00-$25.00. If a fee is required, it will be noted on the application. Keep in mind this fee does not guarantee you a position, or even an interview for that matter. Remember to also send a cover letter and resume along with your application, as noted in the previous chapters.

Some airlines will send you a postcard acknowledging receipt of your application. Other airlines may send you a letter stating they are not currently hiring, but will keep your application on file. If an airline states they will keep your application on file for specific period of time (usually 6 months or 12 months), they really will. If they request that you wait that period of time to reapply...do! They have files on each applicant, and will know if you have submitted more than one application within the specified period. Do not call the airline or show up at their personnel department asking about the status of your application. They will only think you are a nuisance, and it may work to your disadvantage. Some airlines will not respond at all, until they contact you concerning an interview. I know it is difficult to be patient when you are anxious to begin a career, however use the time wisely and continue marketing yourself to other carriers. **Don't put all your eggs in one basket**. The more companies with whom you apply, the greater your chance of receiving a job offer.

So let's say you send off your application, and two weeks later you receive a letter stating you have been selected for an interview. After kissing the mailman, doing a victory dance in the street, and calling your twenty closest friends, you will have to prepare for the big day. Read on to find out what to expect in the strange world of "flight attendant interviews", and how to conquer them.

Notes

Notes

PART IV

How To Conquer The Interviewing Process

Chapter 9

Interviewing -
The Basic Do's And Don'ts

So the day is finally here - time for the big interview! This is your chance to really sell yourself in person and show them why you're the best candidate for the job. The airlines will be looking for people who fit their profile of a perfect flight attendant, evaluating applicants on personality, experience, education, and personal grooming. Before we discuss the different types of interviews you may encounter or the questions you may be asked, I would like to discuss some general do's and don'ts that will apply to the entire interviewing process.

Do's & Don'ts

Do prepare for the interview- know about the company, review the company fact sheets in the Reference section for the major carriers, make a trip to the library, review any information the company has sent you, review the interview questions in Chapter 11.

Do get a good night's sleep before the interview.

Do arrive at the interview **at least** 15-20 minutes early.

Do make a dry run to the interview location (if in town) so you won't get lost.

Do greet the interviewer with a sincere smile, good eye contact, and a firm handshake. Make sure you don't have sweaty hands. Don't fold your hands while waiting for an interview as it can increase sweat build up. You can discretely wipe them on your lap prior to shaking the interviewers hand if they do get sweaty.

Do take a trip to the bathroom prior to your interview. You can take a minute to calm your nerves, use the lavatory (sometimes the interviews last much longer than you had planned so it's best to be prepared), and wash your hands. Make sure you dry them completely so the interviewer isn't greeted with a wet clammy handshake - yuck!

Do remember to **smile** throughout the interview!

Do be extremely attentive during the entire interviewing process, even while others are speaking.

Do carry your credentials in a professional / presentable briefcase or portfolio.

Do keep all answers positive - never make negative comments concerning previous employers, co-workers, job responsibilities, etc.

Do express your sense of humor (however no offensive jokes or nervous laughter).

Do try to relax and show a sense of confidence (remember however that confidence does not equal cockiness).

Do be aware of your strengths and weaknesses and how they relate to the job.

Do be aware of your customer service skills and how they relate to the job.

Do remember to sell yourself.

Do be aware of your body language- sit up straight in your chair, don't cross your arms as it can make you look unapproachable, walk with poise and good posture.

Do try to control fidgeting or signs of nervousness (nail biting / playing with jewelry / profuse sweating).

Do emphasize what you can do for the company, **not** what the company can do for you.

Do get across your strongest assets.

Do bring your pen, pencil, paper, copy of the application (if applicable), extra resumes, copy of birth certificate, passport (if you have one), pertinent information (schools, references, and employers), proof of eligibility to work in the U.S., social security card, and watch.

Do be courteous and friendly to everyone you come in contact with (receptionist, hotel personnel, etc.). There was a United flight attendant who saw an applicant get very intoxicated and belligerent on her flight home from the final interview. The flight attendant reported the applicant; needless to say, she didn't get the job!

Do refer to the interviewer as Mr./Ms./Mrs. unless instructed otherwise.

Do emphasize that you are willing to relocate. You will probably not be hired otherwise.

Don't do the opposites of any of the do's.

Don't be late.

Don't compare yourself to the other applicants.

Don't duplicate the other applicant's responses to questions.

Don't use incorrect grammar when speaking.

Don't allow your attention to wander during the interview while other applicants are speaking.

Don't wear a phony or artificial smile.

Don't chew gum or smoke. This means <u>anywhere</u>, including bathrooms and waiting rooms. Most airlines forbid flight attendants to chew gum on duty. Some airlines only hire non-smokers, and other airlines would prefer to hire non-smokers. Don't give them a reason to eliminate you.

Don't be shy or timid. They want individuals who interact well with others.

Don't answer questions simply with yes or no answers. Elaborate and give examples whenever possible.

Grooming - Women

Do wear conservative clothing, such as a skirted suit or dress.

Do make sure your outfit is clean and pressed.

Do dress in conservative colors such as dark blues, blacks, neutrals. Some suggest you wear the color of the airline's uniforms so that the interviewers can visualize you as one of their flight attendants. It can't hurt!

Do wear pantyhose. Bring an extra pair in anticipation of runs.

Do wear conservative jewelry (no nose rings!). Keep earrings smaller than a quarter, which is the requirement of most airlines for their flight attendants.

Do wear complimentary but not excessive make-up.

Do have clean, well manicured nails (no claws!).

Do have an outfit made of a material that is wrinkle-free (wool blend vs. linen).

Do wear low to medium heels (no 4 inch spikes, Doc Martins, clogs).

Do wear your hair in a conservative style. It doesn't necessarily have to be worn up, but should look professional and neat.

Don't wear excessive perfume. Think of 150 women in a room with too much perfume on- besides you don't want to be remembered for your scent!

Don't wear pants, a pantsuit, shorts, a mini-skirt, etc.

Don't wear fad hairstyles, clothes, jewelry. Keep hair accessories conservative (no 12" bows protruding from your head!)

Don't overdue it on the make-up.

Don't wear tight, revealing clothing. Remember flight attendants today portray a <u>different</u> image!

Grooming - Men

Do wear conservative clothing, such as a dark suit or dress pants and sport coat.

Do wear a conservative silk tie.

Do wear a long sleeve shirt, preferably white or a light pastel.

Do wear shined shoes.

Do have your hair worn no longer than the shirt collar.

Do have your mustache trimmed above your lip and no wider than the mouth (a clean shaven face is preferred by most airlines).

Don't wear an earring.

Don't wear excessive after-shave (for the same reason women shouldn't wear excessive perfume).

Although some of these grooming rules may seem stringent or unfair, it is all part of the package when working for the airlines. You will be expected to conform to uniform standards at all times, and they are looking to hire individuals who will follow their strict (if sometimes stringent or unfair) rules and regulations. Because there is so little supervision in the "real world", the airlines want to hire applicants that they believe will follow their requirements without question or rebellion.

Keep in mind that first impressions are extremely powerful and can never be taken back. Make sure you leave a positive lasting impression of the prepared, well groomed professional that you are.

Notes

Notes

Chapter 10

Types Of Interviews

Flight attendant interviews are unlike any interviews you have probably ever had (or will <u>ever</u> have for that matter!) There are several different types of interviews you may encounter when pursuing a flight attendant career, and they can be broken down into three categories; group/screening, panel, and one-one-one. We will discuss the group interview first, since it is the first type of interview you will have to master.

The Group / Screening Interview

The group/screening interview (otherwise referred to as an Open House) allows the airlines to make a quick, preliminary assessment of a candidate's qualifications. They must decide whether those correspond to the attributes they are looking for in the ideal flight attendant.

Some airlines grant group interviews only to applicants who have sent in a resume or application. Other airlines will advertise the upcoming interview in the classified section of the local paper approximately 1-2 weeks in advance, as was discussed earlier. Some airlines will interview over a period of 2-3 days, while others will only hold interviews on one day. There are usually three time slots, approximately 9:00 AM, 12:00 PM, and 3:00 PM. It is best to interview in the morning or directly after lunch if given a choice. The interviewers are most attentive at these times and you will have the greatest chance of leaving a lasting impression. Also, if you wait for the last time slot, you may <u>not</u> have the opportunity to interview. As noted earlier, if there is a surplus of applicants from earlier in the day, they will have priority over later applicants.

If the airline only holds group/screening interviews at their corporate headquarters and you do not live in that city, the airline will usually provide transportation for you. They will give you a ticket from the closest city to you that they service. However, if the airline is holding Open Houses at several cities around the country, it is your responsibility to get to an interview.

When you arrive for the interview, you will probably be asked to sign in, given a sheet with some basic information about the position such as salary, domicile bases, training, etc., and asked to fill out an information sheet or application (if you have not already filled one out). Take your time and make sure your application/information sheet is as thorough and legible as possible. Once again, it will be much easier if you have the sample application from Chapter 8 with you, as well as the following items:

- ✈ Pen
- ✈ Pencil
- ✈ Paper
- ✈ Extra resumes
- ✈ Copy of your application (if you have already filled one out)
- ✈ Important names, dates, addresses (schools, employers and references)
- ✈ Social security card
- ✈ Copy of your birth certificate
- ✈ Proof of eligibility to work in the U.S.
- ✈ Letter from airlines confirming interview (if applicable)
- ✈ Watch

Once you have completed the paperwork, you will be placed in a room with anywhere from 5-50 applicants. Always try to sit toward the front, as it shows initiative and assertiveness (and that you are not trying to "hide" in the back). Do not be intimidated by the competition. As we discussed earlier, you never know what their qualifications are. They probably just saw the ad in the paper the week before and are totally unprepared, **unlike yourself**. Be confident - you have a reason to be!

Feel free to interact with the other applicants. It can ease tension, and I heard of an airline that actually uses this as a test of the applicant's social skills. The interviewer will ask the applicants questions regarding the other applicants as they enter the interviewing room from the waiting room. I have never personally experienced such an interview; however, you should be aware that you may encounter it. The following exercise is currently being used by a charter airline; the applicants are given a set of instructions to follow such as; go into the room, hang up your coat, circle around the chairs, find the seat with your name on it, sit down, and put all your personal belongings under your seat. They are testing your listening skills, as well as your ability to handle several tasks under stress (not that the tasks are stressful but the interviewing situation definitely is!) with poise.

There will usually be several company representatives from either the In-flight Department or Human Resources Department. They will tell you a little bit about themselves, including their name, job responsibilities, etc. Make sure you write down their name and title so you have the information when writing your thank-you letter. You may also be quizzed on their name during the interview as a test of your listening skills. After the interviewers have been introduced, they will discuss some general information concerning the company as well as the flight attendant position. You will be watched and critiqued from the minute you walk in the door, so be on your best behavior. They are noting your communication skills, the manner in which you carry yourself, your grooming, your ability to interact with others, how well you listen to those around you, etc.

They will usually ask you a simple question and you will be given a time period (ranging from one to three minutes) to give a clear, organized response. Often times, only one or two company representatives will actually ask the questions. The others will be taking notes on the applicant's responses. This may drive you a bit crazy at first, but remember they have a short period of time to make an evaluation. They are attempting to gather as much information as possible on each applicant.

In most situations you will be asked to walk in front of the group to speak, although in some cases you may be asked to stand and speak form where you are sitting. They want to test your poise, your level of self-confidence, and your ability to speak in front of a group. On any given day as a flight attendant, you will be standing in front of hundreds of passengers giving a safety demonstration. They don't want to hire someone who is going to have an anxiety attack once they have a hundred eyes staring at them (It doesn't instill much confidence in the passengers if a flight attendant is shaking and sweating profusely at the front of the cabin prior to take-off!).

Sometimes they will start the questioning at the front of the room, sometimes the back of the room, and sometimes they will call people at random. **Do not** volunteer to be the first to answer a question. If you wait to answer, you will have additional time to gather your thoughts and you will be able to answer the question in a more complete and organized manner. You can also learn from other applicants answers, however never "copy" their responses. Always be attentive to what the other applicants are saying, as you may be asked to expand on what they have just said. This is another way for the interviewers to test your listening skills.

If I could give one piece of advice, it would be to **remember to smile**. While in training at United, we all seemed so diverse that I couldn't figure out what they were using as their selection criteria. After getting to know everyone a little better I finally realized what it was that we all had in common. We all had the ability to smile and appear enthusiastic when we spoke in front of the group. I think everyone can think of someone who may not be drop-dead gorgeous, but they are beautiful to everyone who knows them. It's because they always appear happy and are quick to produce a genuine smile. I don't recommend having a big, artificial grin on your face for the duration of the interview; however, you should try to look as though you are happy and excited to be there.

Actual Questions Asked

During the group interview you will probably be asked one of the following questions:
1) Tell us about yourself ?
2) Why do you want to be a flight attendant? / Why do you want to work for ABC Airlines?/ Why should we hire you?

Let's handle one at a time.
1) Tell us about yourself?

You can use the following list as a guideline to give a complete answer to the question:
1) Name
2) Where you grew up
3) Education
4) Any additional training you have, languages you speak (a big bonus)
5) Extracurricular activities, offices, honors in school
6) Where you are currently working and your job title/responsibilities
7) Previous experience (preferably with customer service, public contact, etc.)
8) Volunteer work, hobbies, clubs, sports
9) Anything else that makes you unique

2) Why do you want to be a flight attendant?/ Why do you want to work for ABC Airlines?/ Why should we hire you?
Don't say "because I love people and love to travel"!
Don't answer in a way that states what the company can do for you (i.e. the travel benefits, days off, etc.).
Don't say "I want the job **sooo** bad" , "I would do **anything** to become a flight attendant", or "I've **always** wanted to be a flight attendant."

Instead you can explain your desire to begin a long term career that offers challenge and variety with a stable, reputable company. You can express your interest in other people, places, and cultures. You can discuss all those traits you possess that just happen to be the traits they are looking for in a good flight attendant (review chapter 3). You can support this statement with examples of previous customer contact positions that you loved and at which you were successful (which also shows you not only enjoy working with people, but are good at interacting with the general public on a daily basis). You may be saying "I love people and love to travel" in a different way; however it is much more unique, believable, and interesting for the interviewers to listen to!

This is also a great time to add any facts you've uncovered while researching the company, such as "I want to work for ABC Airlines, not only because of their strong reputation within the industry, but I read in last months Traveler magazine that ABC Airlines was rated #1 in passenger satisfaction by a survey of frequent fliers. That really impressed me, and I felt as a flight attendant for ABC Airlines I could help contribute to the future success of the company."

Definitely **do not** answer with short, simple responses that will not allow them to see your individuality. You will be shocked and amazed at some of the responses you will hear. I remember one of the questions our group was asked was "Why do you want to work for this airline?" and several people answered "Because you are the only airlines hiring." - Yikes! They may have been right, however keep in mind you need to show the airlines all the skills and traits you have that will benefit **them**. This is your chance to really express your dynamic personality, as well as all the reasons why you will make an excellent flight attendant for their company.

You may want to practice in front of a mirror, into a tape recorder, or in front of family and friends prior to the interview. You might feel sort of goofy at first, but it really does help. Keep in mind you are going to have to stand up in front of a fairly large group, and the more familiar you are with what your going to say, the more comfortable you will appear.

Don't memorize what you want to say word for word, as you **do not** want to sound like you have a canned speech. It does help however to have a general outline of the key points you want to hit, and practice several times to remember the important details. Always remember to speak to the entire room, as well as the panel of interviewers, and always try to establish eye contact. Try to keep your voice calm and steady. You know what to expect and how to answer the questions correctly, so let your confidence shine through. Even if you are nervous, which you more than likely will be, try not to let it show.

Try to exude enthusiasm in your voice, and again, **smile, smile, smile**. Also remember, **it's often not just <u>what</u> you say, but <u>how</u> you say it**. The interviewers hear so many similar responses to their questions that your excitement and spirit will not only set you apart from the crowd, but give the interviewers a much needed jolt. Once you are finished and take your seat, remember to be an active listener for the rest of the applicants.

Selection

Once the group interview is over you may be notified in several ways if you were selected for the next interview. Some airlines actually hold the next interview that same day, directing the chosen applicants to a separate room while the others are released to go home. Most airlines split the interviews however, and will contact you either by phone or letter within one day to several weeks following the initial interview. If the second interview requires travel to their headquarters, that will be provided by the airline. Overnight stay is usually not required.

Remember to send your "thank-you" letters out immediately, expressing your appreciation for their time, as well as reiterating your strong enthusiasm for the position. Make sure to address the letters directly to the interviewers. Also, don't forget to fill out your "Job Log" with all of your new information. Because you were so prepared you (of course) made it to the next step, which is either the panel or one-on-one interview.

Panel / One-On-One Interviews

Most airlines will have at least two interviews, with some having as many as three or four. In most cases, they will consist of either panel or one-on- one interviews. For both the panel and one-on-one interview, you will be alone with the interviewer/interviewers. The difference between the two is that the panel interview will have more than one person doing the interviewing. The interviewers may take turns asking you questions, or like the group interview, only one may ask questions while the others write. In both types of interviews, the questions and scenarios are basically the same. During the group interview the airlines have to make an assessment based on only a brief period of time with you. The panel/one on one interview will allow the interviewers to probe a bit deeper into your previous work experience, educational background, true personality, etc.

To prepare for this interview review your Do's and Don'ts list once again, review the company fact sheets found in the reference section (if interviewing with a major carrier), review the questions from Chapter 11, and review your application. As noted in previous chapters, the airlines are required to do an extremely thorough background check. They will go over your application with you in detail, asking very specific questions regarding your education and employment history. They do not like to see gaps in your employment (they do not count school or any other type of training as a gap) so be prepared with explanations if you fall under this category. If you were self-employed they may ask for proof. Once again, they will be very thorough when checking your background, so always be completely honest. Common questions concerning your previous employment are:

- ✈ What were your job responsibilities?
- ✈ Why did you leave?
- ✈ What kind of a reference would you get?
- ✈ What did you like most/least about the job?

If you left a previous employer under less than pleasant terms, remember to stay positive. You should never criticize a former employer, even if he or she was Atila the Hun. You should never lie; however you can state that you left "to pursue a career as a flight attendant", "to obtain a position that provided greater challenges", "to take a more lucrative position", etc. Always keep your responses positive! Common questions regarding your education are:

- ✈ Why did you choose the school/major you chose?
- ✈ Would you change your decision if you could?
- ✈ What classes did you like most/least?
- ✈ Who paid for your education?
- ✈ Were you involved in any extracurricular activities?
- ✈ What was your grade point average?
- ✈ If you started college but did not finish, what was the reason?

In the next chapter we will discuss these questions, as well as additional questions you may be asked during the interview, and hints on how to answer them.

Testing

You may also be tested during the first or second interview. These tests will measure your skills in basic math, vocabulary, reasoning, and comprehension. It helps to become familiar with military time because there are often questions on the test referring to it. Once again you can find a chart in the Reference section which demonstrates the conversion of the 24 hour clock into military time. You will be given a conversion chart to use for the test, however you will find the test much easier if you are already familiar with it. Listen to all the instructions you are given, and be sure to read the directions carefully. For several of the sections, the instructions and information are supplied. They simply are testing how well you pay attention to details. Some tests will have a time limit. If that is the case, make sure to write down by what time you must have the test completed. This will help you to utilize your time wisely and keep track of the amount of time remaining.

Group Exercises

During the second interview you may also be given a "group exercise" to see how well you work and interact with others. This is an example of one exercise that is currently being used. You will be given a list of twenty adjectives that describe a flight attendant and told to individually eliminate ten, so that the most important ten are remaining. Then you will get together as a group and discuss why you each chose your ten adjectives. Then as a group you must choose and agree on the ten most important adjectives.

The ten words the group chooses are not as important as how the group works together to achieve their final results. The interviewers will be watching each applicant to see how they interact with the group. They are looking for people who can communicate their opinions without being too dominating or submissive. They usually ask for a "group leader" and it is in your favor to volunteer for this position. It shows initiative and a willingness to take charge. As a group leader, you want to get everyone involved and direct the group without being too quiet or too overbearing.

Video Scenarios

At some stage of the interviewing process, you may also be asked to watch a series of scenarios on video. You will be shown approximately forty-five minutes of customer service situations and asked to rank the flight attendants performances from poor to excellent. The scenarios are pretty basic and it is a fairly easy exercise. Just remember to always take the view of the passenger, and rate the flight attendant in the scenario based on how you would feel you were being treated as the customer.

If all goes well, you will breeze through the second (third, fourth) interview and move on to the next step. You will usually be notified by letter or phone if the company wants you to continue on to the next stage, which is the company physical. With some airlines, the physical will actually be given on the same day. At this point, if you pass your physical and your background check is acceptable, you will be given a training date.

If you are not invited to a second (third, fourth) interview or do not get a job offer, **do not get discouraged**. The competition for flight attendant positions is very fierce. If you have followed all the necessary steps, then you have done all that you can do. Most airlines will not tell you why you were not hired. Unfortunately it is often out of your hands. Although the interview process is supposed to be objective, it's impossible to expect complete objectivity anytime you're dealing with human beings with different personalities. I had a friend who was not only the best flight attendant I'd known, but he also had experience as a flight attendant trainer and supervisor. He was not hired by a major carrier; however, several other people I knew, who were much less qualified, were hired. Sometimes you just don't fit an interviewer's mental image of the "perfect flight attendant", and nothing you can say or do will change that.

You must remain positive and believe the next company with which you interview will be a better fit. You must learn from any previous mistakes, and then move on. You have to think of it as an excellent investment of your time, keeping in mind that your interviewing skills will improve with each experience. If you had your heart set on one particular company, you can usually re-apply within 6-12 months. I have known people who originally were not hired by a particular carrier, however reapplied and were hired a year later. I would suggest however, to continue your search with other companies. There are many airlines and you will find the right one for you. **The only way you can fail is if you stop trying**!

Notes

Chapter 11

The Most Commonly Asked
Interview Questions

In this chapter you will find a list of questions that are currently being asked most frequently by the airlines, as well as hints on how to answer them. Some questions have been grouped together because their responses are similar. Remember once again, they are looking for the traits we covered in Chapter 3 "What The Airlines Are Looking For In A Flight Attendant". Keep this chapter in mind when considering your response to the following questions.

1) What kind of flight attendant will you be? / What qualities do you think make a good flight attendant?
Hint: Review the list of desired Personality Traits in Chapter 3.

2) Give a customer service situation in which you made a difference? / Describe a time when you had someone angry with you and how you handled it?
Hint: If you do not have paid customer service experience, you can use volunteer work, church activities, etc.

3) What do you like most about your current job?
Hint: Discuss traits that would also be found in the flight attendant position. Example: variety, the opportunity to work with all types of personalities, travel, etc.

4) What do you like least about your current job?
Hint: Remember to answer "negative" questions with a "positive" , such as "I wish I had an opportunity to interact with people more."

5) What have you done to prepare for this interview? / What do you know about ABC Airlines?
Hint: Review the company fact sheets in the reference section, take a trip to the library, interview flight attendants, review the list of additional sources of information in the Reference section, etc.

6) What are your strengths? / Describe yourself using three adjectives. / How would you describe yourself? / What is your best trait?
Hint: Review the list of desired Personality Traits in Chapter 3.

7) What are your weakness? / What are you trying to improve on? / What would you change about yourself?
Hint: Turn a negative question into a positive - Example: overachiever, expect too much of yourself, hold the same high expectations for others as you do for yourself, etc.

8) What do you think are the primary responsibilities of a flight attendant?
Hint: The primary responsibility of a flight attendant is **safety**. The secondary responsibilities are providing comfort and service to the passengers.

9) How do you feel about working on weekends, holidays, and nights?
Hint: Express your flexibility and awareness that this is part of the job. Example; I am aware of the diverse schedule of a flight attendant, and I look forward to the variety that this type of position provides.

10) Are you willing to relocate?
Hint: The only acceptable answer is yes.

11) Why do you want to leave your present employer?
Hint: Don't state the negatives concerning your current job. Instead reiterate your strong desire to pursue a career as a flight attendant.

12) **How do you feel about conforming to our uniform standards? / Being told how to dress? /Being told how to wear your hair?/Being told how to wear your make-up?**
Hint: The airlines are big on conformity due to the fact that there is so little supervision out in the "real world". Express complete compliance with any of their rules and regulations.

13) **What will you like the most about this job?**
Hint: Keep in mind what you can do for the company, <u>not</u> what the company can do for you. Example; Instead of stating the travel benefits or days off, you should state the opportunity to use your human relations skills in a long term career that provides variety, along with the opportunity to meet and work with new and interesting people.

14) **What will you like the least?**
Hint: Again try to answer a negative question with a positive response. Example: That my friends and family will not be able to share in the unique adventure I will be experiencing.

15) **Give an example of a recent situation that you disagreed with a co-worker? How did you handle it?**
Hint: Show your maturity and ability to get along with others. They are looking for someone who can confront an individual in a diplomatic manner and get the problem resolved. There are no supervisors at 30,000 feet!

16) **How many days of work did you miss due to illness last year? / What do you consider to be good attendance?**
Hint: Attendance is a very important issue in the airline industry due to the nature of the job. They are looking for people who will provide perfect attendance and who demonstrate a good attendance record in the past.

17) **What kind of recommendations / references would you get from your previous employers?**
Hint: They are looking for people with strong employment histories that have the ability to get along with others, especially those in authority.

18) **Where do you see yourself in 5 years?**
Hint: If you have aspirations of moving into management or another department you can state that. Flight attendants have opportunities to go into a variety of positions such as In-flight supervisor, trainer, recruiter, sales, marketing, public relations, etc. If you desire a long-term career as a flight attendant however, let them know. They will spend a great deal of time and money training you and like to know you plan on sticking around. You can express your enthusiasm about becoming a flight attendant, and that in five years you see yourself as an experienced flight attendant with many more years of service to contribute.

19) Can you live off the salary you were quoted?

Hint: Confirm that you will not quit two weeks after training when you are tired of living off of peanut butter and jelly sandwiches. Assure them you have created a budget, and that you will be able to meet your expenses.

20) How will your personal relationships be affected by this job? / How would your family feel about you taking this position? / If hired, what personal adjustments in your life would you expect to be necessary?

Hint: The interviewers want to know that you are aware of the unique requirements of this position and that you have full support from friends and family.

21) What do you do in your free time? / What are your hobbies or interests?

Hint: They are looking for people who are well rounded and active. Watching television or playing video games will not score big points here.

22) What type of passenger would you like to deal with most? / least?

Hint: This is another opportunity to express how much you enjoy dealing with the public. Example; In my previous positions I have always enjoyed the variety of personalities with which I was able to interact, and I feel it would be the same as an employee of ABC Airlines. Once again, turn a negative into a positive.

23) How would your friends describe you? / How would a stranger describe you?

Hint: Review the list of desired Personality Traits in Chapter 3.

24) What is my name?

Hint: This is a test of your listening skills. If possible, write the interviewers names down when you are introduced. This is important for writing thank you notes after the interview as well. It is also a bonus to remember their name, so after the interview you can thank them using their name (remember to use Mr., Mrs., or Ms.). They will be impressed with your memory and professionalism.

25) When can you start training?

Hint: The airlines will not only understand that you will need to give your current employer two weeks notice, they will expect it from you. It shows maturity and professionalism to give your previous employer two weeks notice. If you are not currently employed, you can state "immediately".

26) What is your greatest achievement?

Hint: This is a wonderful chance to shine (awards, putting yourself through college, athletic achievements, social service, etc.)

27) How is this position like previous jobs you have had?

Hint: Review the first two chapters and relate previous jobs to the responsibilities of a flight attendant (customer service, food service, human relation skills)

28) **Give an example of a time you had to take time out of your day to explain something to someone.**
Hint: This is an opportunity to show your customer relations and communication skills, as well as your patience and ability to handle multiple tasks.

29) **What was the last book you read? / What is your favorite book?**
Hint: They are looking for individuals who are well rounded and knowledgeable. Stay away from comic books and Harlequin Romance novels and you should be fine.

30) **Have you ever lived away from home?**
Note: If you have, great. If not, assure them that you are emotionally prepared to move away and begin your career.

31) **Give an example of a time you had to follow a policy/rule you did not believe in.**
Hint: Because the industry is strictly mandated by FAA rules and regulations, the airlines want to be sure they are hiring someone who would not have a problem following them, even if you may question their necessity or validity. Again, since there is little supervision in the real world, they have to be assured that they are hiring individuals who will comply with the rules without being constantly monitored.

32) **Are you a leader or follower? / Do you like to be in charge?**
Hint: The airlines want someone who can take charge in the unlikely event that an emergency situation were to occur. Also, because there are no supervisors 30,000 feet in the air, flight attendants have to be able to take charge of challenging situations.

33) **What is the ideal job? / Ideal workday?**
Hint: Review Chapters 1&2. Mention the qualities that the flight attendant job offers; variety, customer interaction, travel, chance to help others, meet people, etc.

34) **Do people like you?**
Hint: Of course you will say yes, but follow that up with examples proving it; elected student body president, got along extremely well with co-workers, letters of praise from previous customers, strong references from supervisors, etc.

35) **How would you handle an intoxicated passenger? / A scared passenger? / An irate passenger?**
Hint: They are looking for people who will deal with daily challenges in a mature and professional manner.

36) **How do you deal with stress? / Do you like to juggle several tasks at once?**
Hint: Express positive methods of dealing with stress such as exercise, yoga, relaxation techniques, positive attitude. They are looking for people who can keep their cool in stressful situations.

37) Are you a day or night person? / Have you ever had a problem with a schedule you had to work?

Hint: Let the interviewer know you are well aware of the variety in the work schedules and are looking forward to the unique work conditions.

38) Why did you choose the school/major you chose? Would you change your decision?

Hint: This is a good question for the interviewers to get to know you better and learn of your interests. **Don't say** because your parents made you chose a certain major, or it was the only school/major you could get into!

39) What was your grade point average? Do you feel this was a good representation of your efforts?

Hint: Do not lie about your grade point average - it is very easy to check. If you had bad grades, you should have some explanation to offer. Example; "I took on too much, holding down two jobs while attending school. If I had it to do over again, I would plan ahead financially so I could invest the amount of time an education requires." If you had average grades you can express that you feel you received a well-rounded educational experience, balancing classes with extracurricular activities.

40) Who paid for your education?

Hint: If you put yourself through school, that is a great achievement you should let them know about. If you earned a scholarship in academics or athletics, again that is a great accomplishment you should make the interviewer aware of. If you were fortunate enough to have assistance from your parents, express your appreciation for such a gift.

41) What question did you think I would ask and didn't, and how would you answer it?

Hint: Pick something you are comfortable with. If you feel knowledgeable about the company, pick "What do you know about our airline?" You are sure to impress them with the effort you took to learn about the carrier prior to the interview. You would be surprised how many people don't!

42) Of all the bases available, choose the one you want to go to least. Explain if you were based there how you would handle it and how you would prepare to go.

Hint: Once again they want to know you are willing to relocate **anywhere,** and to make sure you have thought about the consequences of being in a city that was not your first choice. Reiterate that you are aware of the relocation requirements of a flight attendant position, and that you are looking forward to the adventure. Choose a city, and then tell how you would prepare for your new residence by learning what unique benefits that city has to offer, making the most out of your time there.

43) When people first meet you, what is a misconception they have of you?

Hint: Keep it positive. Such as "Sometimes when I am in deep thought I get a serious look on my face. People might not realize what an easy going person I am."

44) How would you handle a co-worker who was not pulling their share of the load?

Hint: Again, they are testing your ability to handle conflict. Express your maturity by discussing the matter with the co-worker in a diplomatic manner.

Potential Questions To Ask The Interviewer

✈ Is there anything I can do now to better prepare myself for training?

✈ Is there a limit to the hours per month I can work?

✈ Where does the company see itself in the next five years? Ask if they are planning to enter a market you know they are currently not servicing, showing you are aware of their current route structure.

✈ What percentage of the base is on reserve?

✈ How soon after training will I be expected to report to my base?

✈ How soon will I be notified of your hiring decision?

Notes

Notes

PART V

How To Survive
Flight Attendant
Training

Chapter 12

Training Program Outline

Much like the interviewing process, flight attendant training is unlike anything you will ever experience again. As a recent college graduate, I felt passing the training program meant basically just showing up. How hard can it be to learn to make a few drinks and say "bye-bye". Right? --Wrong! I didn't realize that you are not an employee of the company until you successfully pass training. And not everyone does! It is actually a very challenging program that only those who follow the rules and apply themselves will pass. This chapter will explain the training process, so that you are prepared and know what will be expected of you.

Prior to training you will receive a packet from the airline, which will give you a great deal of pertinent information. You will receive details on the length of training, your transportation to training, directions to the training facility once you arrive, the type of clothing you will need to bring to training, an outline of the training program, and several subjects you must learn prior to your arrival. The training programs cover the following subjects:

✈ **General Airline Knowledge / Company Information**
✈ **Emergency Procedures / First Aid Training**
✈ **Personal Grooming / Appearance**
✈ **Customer Service / Flight Attendant Responsibilities**
✈ **Food / Beverage Service**

Length of Training

Training programs can range from 2-8 weeks, depending on the size of the carrier and the variety of aircraft in their fleet. The major carriers tend to have the most extensive training, usually lasting six weeks or more. We'll be discussing the major airlines' training program since it is the most challenging, and the requirements will be similar to the other types of carriers.

Compensation

Most of the airlines provide transportation to training, lodging, and meals (or a meal allowance called per diem) during the training program. Some airlines will pay you while in training, and some will not. Therefore you will need to plan ahead financially for fixed expenses, such as car payments and credit cards. The only major airline that is currently charging for training is TWA.

You will need to have enough money saved for incidental expenses, such as toiletry items or eating out occasionally. You may be sent to your new domicile directly after training, so you might want to have money set aside for your new residence (i.e. deposit on an apartment, etc.) The training is usually held in the same city as the airline's headquarters, and the lodging and classrooms will usually be in a hotel or a training center.

Testing

You will be tested several times a week, and you will have to maintain a specific grade point average, usually between 85-90%. You will be occupied with some form of training 6 days a week, 8-10 hours a day, for approximately 6 weeks. If it sounds challenging, that's because it is!

The airlines are regulated by the FAA (Federal Aviation Administration). As with any government agency, they have outdone themselves in the number of rules and regulations they have created pertaining to flight attendants. You must be familiar with all of these rules as well as required emergency procedures and emergency equipment (also mandated by the FAA). When you throw in CPR and basic first aid training, aircraft familiarization, basic airline lingo and information, a variety of meal/beverage services, safety announcements, customer service skills and role-playing, personal grooming, and company policies, it makes for a busy 6 weeks.

You will gain all of this knowledge in a variety of ways. It will be split up between classroom lecture, role playing, hands-on training, self-instructional workbooks, and possibly learning centers. Most training programs now have learning centers, which offer individual work stations with computers and video screens. The lessons are self-instructional and can be done at your own pace. Prior to graduation you will also have at least five hours (minimum required by FAA) of actual hands on experience as a flight attendant. Sometime during training you will be assigned a trip to work, giving you an opportunity to see what the job actually entails and to apply what you have been learning.

One of the most challenging weeks of training is emergency procedures / first aid training. This is when you realize what your job is all about and why you are really there. Some airlines use simulators for their emergency drills. Simulators are airplane mock-ups that have the capacity to simulate a crash, fire, block exits, and produce smoke. In these mock-ups you are able to role-play different emergency situations and practice your evacuation drills in an extremely realistic setting. You will not only need to pass emergency procedures during training, but you will be tested every year for the duration of your career as a flight attendant.

Required Dress

You will be expected to dress in business attire every day, unless notified otherwise. You will be given a list of the rules and regulations regarding the dress code on the first day, and will be expected to follow it for the duration of the training period. The regulations will mirror those required of the airline's active flight attendants. The purpose is to allow individuals to get used to the rules while in training, so they become second nature once you are out in the real world. It is also an opportunity to weed out those people that have a problem staying within the required guidelines.

Uniforms

During training you will also be fitted for your uniforms. Most carriers charge the employees for the first set of uniforms, and provide replacement pieces for free. The cost usually ranges from $600.00-$800.00, and can be paid through monthly payroll deductions of $25.00- $50.00. The initial uniform package usually consists of any three bottom pieces (skirt, dress, pant), 4-6 blouses or shirts, a blazer, belt, a purse for women, luggage, and a coat. You will be given a list of appropriate shoe styles and will be responsible for purchasing your own shoes.

Domicile Assignment

You will also be given your new domicile while in training. In most situations you will have a choice between several cities, however not always. The choices will vary, depending on where flight attendants are needed most within the system. Airlines will assign seniority within a class based on either age or social security numbers. Everyone will bid for their domicile choices, and the bases will be awarded based on seniority. If you do get based in a city that is not your first choice, you can usually request a domicile transfer after six months.

Rules and Regulations

Much like the interviewing process, you will be critiqued while in the training program. They will be assessing your ability to get along with others, adherence to the appearance standards, promptness, attitude, communication skills, and class participation. The airlines use the training programs as an extension of the interview process, assessing whether you have the qualities they expect in their flight attendants. Again, they have to weed out individuals who they feel are not good candidates, as there is little chance to monitor them out in the real world. Most airlines have a probation period that lasts approximately six months after training. During this time the airlines will watch newly hired flight attendants particularly close to note any problems with attendance, dealing with passengers, getting along with crew members, etc. Due to the fact that most airlines are unionized, it is very difficult to fire someone after they become an "official flight attendant", after they are off probation.

Well that's basically the nuts and bolts of training. The following chapter, however, gives more of an insider's view of the training experience and how to increase your chances of survival!

Notes

Notes

Chapter 13

What Training Is
Really Like

The two hardest parts to being a flight attendant are getting hired and going through training. Unfortunately you need to survive these two processes before you can reap all the wonderful benefits of being a flight attendant. When you arrive at the training facility you will be full of apprehension, as well as feeling overwhelmed. You will be assigned a room, which you will probably have to share with 1-3 other people. These people will either become your closest friends or a huge thorn in your side, depending on whether your personalities click or not. Remember you will be co-habitating with these people for up to six weeks, so you must make a concerted effort to get along. If you do not bond with your roommates, there will surely be others from your training class with whom you will have something in common. Most classes have between 30-50 individuals that span a wide range of ages, backgrounds, and personalities. The stressful environment, combined with the isolation from friends and family, make it extremely important to have others with whom you can share your experience. Flight attendant training is its own form of boot camp (fondly referred to as Barbie Boot Camp by those who have survived!) and you will form bonds of friendship that will last a lifetime.

Always Be On Your Best Behavior

If you thought you were "on stage" during the interviewing process, that was just the beginning. Training is an extension of the elimination process. You are not officially hired by the airline until you have graduated from their training program. For the duration of the program you will be under a microscope. During my first week of training, I was sitting in a classroom and got the strange feeling I was being watched. I looked to the back of the classroom, only to discover one of our trainers taking notes on us. Talk about Big Brother watching! There were rumors that they had hidden cameras in all of our rooms, as well as in the study rooms! Looking back however, I do believe it was just our overactive imaginations wreaking havoc on our weary bodies. Needless to say, you are constantly being judged, so you should never let your guard down.

Your conduct will be monitored during your entire stay at the training facility. You will usually be given one day off per week, normally a Saturday or Sunday. It is important to take breaks from the facility and from studying, simply for sanity sake. However, save the wild weekends until after training. Two girls from my training class came home during the wee hours, drunk as skunks and whooping it up in the hallways on one of our "off " nights. Not only did our entire training class hear them, but unfortunately so did our instructors. Needless to say, they were removed the next day. Chances are you will have so many layovers in that particular city in the future, you will have more than enough time to take full advantage of all it has to offer. Once again, it is not worth risking a career over.

Study, Study, Study!

As mentioned earlier, you will have tests approximately every other day on the information you have just received, and you must maintain a specific score. If you were given something to learn prior to training, **learn it**. You will be tested on the information the first few days of class, and if you fail you may be sent home immediately. Most airlines will want you to know military time and the city codes. One regional airline requires trainees to memorize all their announcements prior to attending training. You will have so much more information to memorize once you get to training, you need to have any required material under your belt before you arrive. Every night is like a final exam cram session, filling your brain to capacity and then some. Just when you are ready to celebrate a passing score, it's on to the next batch of information to be memorized. You will usually get minimal sleep at night, with only one day a week off. There is a constant fear of whether you will pass or be sent home (imagine telling your friends you flunked Flight Attendant Training!). It's not that the information is difficult -

- there is just a great deal of it to learn in a short period of time. We lost an average of three people a week. It was always difficult to see people with whom you had formed friendships, be released. However, if you keep up with the information you are given and pay attention in class, you should have no problems passing.

Follow The Rules

In the previous chapter we discussed the appearance standards, which should be covered in greater detail. You will be given a set of rules you will be required to follow in the training program, as well as once you are a working flight attendant. This is why you are asked questions during the interviewing process concerning your ability to comply with rules and regulations. Training is very expensive for the airlines, and they try to eliminate those who may have a problem conforming to the requirements.

When I was in training, they would give **one warning** for an appearance standard violation If it happened again, you were dismissed! One rule was that skirts couldn't be any shorter than one inch above the knee. One of my classmates was warned about wearing her skirts too short but continued to wear them, and she was sent home-- no ifs, ands, or buts! The women were also not allowed to wear earrings larger than a quarter. The trainers would actually hold a quarter up to your earrings to measure them, and would write you up if they were in excess. Some carriers check everyone's fingernails on a regular basis to make sure they are properly manicured, and some will require the women to present their make-up and skin care products for approval. Most will require the women to keep their hair restrained away from their face (you will be dealing with food, and therefore will need your hair restrained to meet sanitary requirements). Once again, you are only given one warning to comply and the next step is dismissal. Although there were not as many rules for men, they were required to wear business attire, refrain from wearing earrings, keep their hair cut no longer than the shirt collar, maintain a clean shaven face, etc. Some of these things may seem silly, but it's not worth loosing an incredible career over something as ridiculous as short skirts or large earrings - this is not the time to be a rebel!

Watch Your Attitude

Do not cross your instructors - with one altercation, you may be gone. The trainers are there to make sure you know the necessary information when you graduate, but they are also there to weed out people who may cause conflict with their co-workers. If they feel you have an attitude problem with them or your classmates, you may be sent home without any warning. You are given warnings on appearance violations because they feel it is something you can change; however, an attitude problem is something that cannot be corrected in six weeks. Make a concerted effort to get along with everybody!

During training you will also have aircraft familiarization training, in which you actually get on the planes and become more familiar with the physical location of the items you have been studying. This would be great, except we were taken to the planes at midnight and were there for several hours. I was told later that this was done to see how we functioned at all hours of the night. On reserve you may be called for "all-nighters" (flights between midnight and 6:00 AM), and they don't want people representing their company who completely "snap" when working odd hours. So even if you'd give anything to be home in bed, you have to act like there's no place more exciting than a Boeing 767 at 2:00 AM.

Always Be On Time

Promptness is also extremely important. Once again, this is why you were asked questions during the interviewing process concerning your punctuality. You will be given a class schedule and you will be expected to be on time every day. If you are late, it will be noted. If it is a constant problem, you may be sent home. Because of the nature of the job, they can't have people who are continually late.

Well, those are the rules. If you opt to follow them, you should make it through with flying colors. You will be shocked at how fast the weeks fly by and how much knowledge you will have gained in such a short period of time. On graduation day you will be very proud of your accomplishments and extremely excited to begin your new career. Usually you will be given time after training to organize your life and prepare for your new domicile, if relocation is necessary. However, you may be sent to your new base immediately, so be prepared to apply all that you have learned within 48 hours of graduation! You will usually be given hotel accommodations for the first week or two, but it can still be a pretty crazy transition. While your learning your new job and flying in and out of a new city, you will need to find a place to live, have your things sent to you, etc.

It may seem overwhelming, but somehow it all gets done. Before you know it you will be a seasoned pro, training will be just a blur, and you won't believe you were so stressed out about how to prepare a galley! You're finally able to use all those incredible benefits - you'll get so spoiled that you'll insist on flying to New York City every time you need a haircut, San Francisco for really great bread, and the Orient for your Christmas shopping! You'll get so accustomed to having two weeks off each month, you'll find it impossible to believe you once worked for two weeks off a year! Chances are you'll become one of the 73% of flight attendants who plan on working for their present employer until retirement!

Closing

You should now feel confident to go out and conquer your flight attendant job search. You know what to expect from the job, what the airlines are looking for, the type of airline you want to work for, how to apply and interview, and how to get through training. Have confidence in yourself! You are miles beyond your competition -- now you must put your new knowledge to work.

Without effort and persistence, this new information is useless, and you will be no further ahead than when you started. Take action today and you are one step closer to an exciting and rewarding career as a flight attendant. Paris is waiting! I hope you are able to obtain your dreams and join the ranks of thousands of flight attendants who would never consider doing anything else!

Notes

Reference

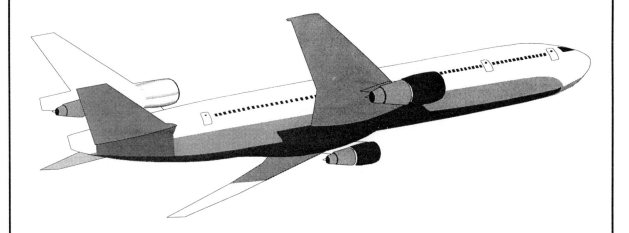

Airline Directory

Major Airlines

Alaska Airlines
P.O. Box 68900
Seattle, WA 98168-0900
Corporate headquarters # - (206) 433-3200
Job hotline # - (206) 433-3230
Sales - $1.1 billion
Employees- 6,900

America West Airlines
4000 East Sky Harbor Blvd.
Phoenix, AZ 85034
Corporate headquarters # - (602) 693-0800
Job hotline # - (602) 693-8650
Sales - $1.4 billion
Employees - 11,600

American Airlines, Inc.
Flight Attendant Recruitment
P.O. Box 619410 Mail Drop 4125
Dallas/Ft. Worth Airport, TX 75261-9410
Corporate headquarters # - (817) 963-1234
Job hotline # - (817) 963-1100 or (817) 963-1110
Corporate Information # - 1-800-267-6177
Sales - $7.2 billion
Employees - 90,000

Continental Airlines, Inc.
Continental Airlines Staffing Office
P.O. Box 60307
Attn: GTW-EP
Houston, TX 77205
Corporate headquarters # - (713) 834-5000
Job hotline # - (713) 834-5300   (6683)
Sales - $5.3 billion   1800-443 8814
Employees - 36,300

Delta Airlines, Inc.
Employment Office
P.O. Box 20530
Hartsfield Atlanta Int'l. Airport
Atlanta, GA 30320 $\quad$ 2501 – DIRECTLY
Corporate headquarters # -(404) 715-2600
Sales - $8.1 billion
Employees - 73,000

Northwest Airlines, Inc.
5101 Northwest Drive
Mail Stop - A1410
St. Paul, MN 55111-3034
Corporate headquarters # - (612) 726-2111
Job hotline # - (612) 726-3600
Sales - $7.3 billion
Employees - 44,000

Southwest Airlines
P.O. Box 36644
Dallas, TX 75235-1644
Attn: People Department
Corporate headquarters # -(214) 792-4000
Job hotline # - (214) 792-4803 $\quad$ 4838
Sales - $2.3 billion
Employees - 16,818

Trans World Airlines
Flight Attendant Division
11495 Natural Bridge Rd. Suite 214
St. Louis, MO 63044
Corporate headquarters # - (314) 589-3000
Job hotline # - (314) 895-6699
Sales - $3.4 billion
Employees - 24,000

United Airlines
Flight Attendant Employment
P.O. Box 66100
Chicago, IL 60666
Corporate headquarters # - (847) 700-4000
Job hotline # - (847) 700-7200
Sales - $11.7 billion
Employees - 78,371

USAir, Inc.
Employee Relations
2345 Crystal Drive
Arlington, VA 22227
Corporate headquarters # - (703) 418-7000
Job hotline # for East Coast- (703) 418-7499
Job hotline # for Northest - (412) 472-7693
Job hotline # for Charlotte area - (704) 359-3200
Job hotline # for the rest of the US - (910) 661-5341
Sales - $6.5 billion
Employees - 44,000

Regional Airlines

Air South, Inc.
P.O. Box 11129
Columbia, SC 29204
Attn: Human Resources
Corporate headquarters # - (803) 822-0502
Job hotline # - 1-800-556-6773
Employees - 550

Air 21
P.O. Box 7797
Fresno, CA 93747-7797
Attn: Flight Attendant Recruitment
Corporate headquarters # - (209) 348-2700

Airtran Airways
6280 Hazeltine National Drive
Orlando, FL 32822
Attn: Inflight Department
Corporate headquarters # - (407) 859-1579
Employees - 185

Aloha Airlines, Inc.
P.O. Box 30028
Honolulu, HI 96820
Attn: Human Resources Dept.
Corporate headquarters # - (808) 836-4101
Job hotline # - (808) 836-4109
Sales - $226 million
Employees - 1,945

Frontier Airlines
12015 E. 46th Avenue Suite 200
Denver, CO 80239
Attn: Human Resources
Corporate headquarters # - (303) 371-7400
Job hotline # - (303) 371-7400 Ext. 1505
Employees - 197

Hawaiian Airlines, Inc.
P.O. Box 30008
Honolulu, HI 96820
Attn: Human Resources Dept.
Corporate headquarters # - (808) 835-3700
Job hotline # (808) 835-3700 - ask operator to connect you
Sales - $331 million
Employees - 2,300

Midwest Express Airlines, Inc.
Midwest Express Recruiting
6744 S. Howell Ave.- HQ-22
Oak Creek, WI 53154
Corporate headquarters # - (414) 570-4000
Job hotline # - (414) 570-4065
Sales - $165 million
Employees - 1,200

Reno Air, Inc.
220 Edison Way
Reno, NV 89052
Corporate headquarters # - (702) 686-3835
Job hotline # - (702) 686-3864
Employees - 420

Spirit Airlines
18121 E. Eight Mile Road, Suite 100
Eastpointe, MI 48021
Corporate headquarters # - (810) 779-2700
Employees - 350
Sales - $50 million

US Air Shuttle
P.O. Box 710616
Laguardia Airport
Flushing, NY 11371
Corporate headquarters # - (718) 397-6062
Employees - 650
Sales - 180 million

Valujet Airlines, Inc.
1800 Phoenix Blvd. Suite 126
Atlanta, GA 30349
Corporate headquarters # - (770) 994-8258
Job hotline # - (770) 994-6235
Employees - 387

Vanguard Airlines
30 Northwest Rome Circle
Kansas City Int'l Airport Terminal B
Kansas City, MO 64153
Attn: Human Resources
Corporate headquarters # - (816) 243-2100

Western Pacific Airlines
2864 S. Circle Drive
Colorado Springs, CO 80906
Corporate headquarters # - (719) 579-7737
Job holinte # - (719) 527-7160

Charter Airlines

American Trans Air, Inc.
Flight Attendant Recruitment
P.O. Box 51609
Indianapolis, IN 46251
Corporate headquarters # - (317) 247-4000
Job hotline # - (317) 240-7106
Sales - $422 million

Carnival Airlines
1815 Griffin Rd. Suite 205
Dania, Fl. 33004
Attn: Personnel Dept.
Corporate headquarters # - (954) 923-8672
Job hotline # - (954) 923-8672 ext.9
Sales - $142 million
Employees - 1,000

Evergreen Int'l Airlines
3850 Three Mile Lane
McMinnville, OR 97128
Attn: Personnel
Corporate headquarters # -(503) 472-0011

Express One Int'l Airlines
3890 W. Northwest Hwy. Suite 700
Dallas, TX 75220
Attn: Recruiting
Corporate headquarters # - (214) 902-2500

Miami Air
P.O. Box 660880
Miami Springs, FL 33266-0880
Corporate headquarters # - (305) 871-3300
Sales - $40 million
Employees - 160

Rich Int'l Airways
P.O. Box 522067
Miami, FL 33152
Corporate headquarters # - (305) 871-5113
Sales - $90 million
Employees - 500
Fax # - (305) 871-3461

Ryan Int'l Airlines
6810 West Kellogg
Wichita, KS 67209
Corporate headquarters # - (316) 942-0141
Employees - 475
Sales - $50 million

Sierra Pacific Airlines
7700 N. Business Park Drive
Tucson, AZ 85743-9622
Corporate headquarters # - (602) 744-1144

Sun Country Airlines, Inc.
2520 Pilot Knob Rd. Suite 250
St. Paul, MN 55120
Attn: Personnel
Corporate headquarters # - (612) 726-5252
Job hotline # - (612) 681-4877 ext 1
Sales - $140 million
Employees - 500

Tower Air
Building #17 - JFK Int'l Airport
Jamaica, NY 11430
Corporate headquarters # - (718) 553-4300
Fax # - (718) 553-4312
Sales -$ 240 million
Employees - 1,400

Viscount Air Services
1000 E. Valencia
Tucson, AZ 85706
Corporate headquarters # - (602) 889-4671
Sales - $36 million
Employees - 250

World Airways
13873 Park Center Rd. Suite 490
Herndon, VA 22071
Attn: Human Resources Department
Corporate headquarters # - (703) 834-9200
Job hotline # - (703) 834-9230
Sales - $200 million
Employees - 750

Commuter Airlines

Air Wisconsin / United Express
W6390 Challenger Drive Suite 203
Appleton, WI 54915-9120
Attn: Employment Opportunities
Corporate headquarters # - (414) 739-5123
Job hotline # - (414) 749-4223
Employees - 600

Allegheny Commuter Airlines / US Air Express
1000 Rosedale Ave. Suite B
Middletown, PA 17057
Attn: Human Resources / Flight Attendant Recruitment
Corporate headquarters # - (717) 944-2781
Fax # - (717) 948-1912 - Can fax your resume and cover letter
Employees - 1,500

Atlantic Coast Airlines / United Express
One Export Drive
Sterling, VA 20164
Corporate headquarters # - (703) 406-6500
Job hotline # - (703) 406-7486
Fax # - (703) 406-7466 - Can fax your resume and cover letter

Atlantic Southeast Airlines, Inc. / Delta Connection
100 Hartsfield Centre Pkwy. Suite 800
Atlanta, GA 30354-1356
Corporate headquarters # - (404) 766-1400
Job hotline # - (404) 766-1400 ask operator to connect you
Sales - $288 million
Employees - 2,109

Business Express / Delta Connection
14 Aviation Avenue
Portsmouth, NH 03801
Corporate headquarters # - (603) 334-4000
Sales - $210 million
Employees - 1,500

CC Air / U S Air Express
4700 Yorkmont Road, Second Floor
Charlotte, NC 28208
Corporate headquarters # - (704)359-8990
Sales - $62 million
Employees - 600

Comair Inc.
P.O. Box 75021
Cincinnati/Northern Kentucky Int'l Airport
Cincinnati, OH 45275
Corporate headquarters # - (606) 767-2550
Sales - $296 million
Employees - 2500

Continental Express
Flight Attendant Recruiting
15333 JFK Blvd. Suite 600
Houston, TX 77032
Corporate headquarters # - (713) 985-2700
Job hotline # - (713) 834-5300
Employees - 2,700

Flagship Airlines / American Eagle
American Eagle Recruitment
P.O. Box 619415 Mail Drop 4121
Ft. Worth, TX 76155-9415
Corporate headquarters # - (805) 541-1010
Job hotline # - (805) 541-1010 ext.8
Employees - 5,000

Great Lakes Airlines / United Express
7900 Xexes Ave. South Suite 190
Bloomington, MN 55431
Attn: Human Resources
Corporate headquarters # - (612)767-7000
Sales - $75 million
Employees - 657

Horizon Air
Horizon Air Employment
P.O. Box 48309
Seattle, WA 98148
Corporate headquarters # - (206) 241-6757
Job hotline # - (206) 248-6334
Employees - 2,000

Mountain West Airlines / Mesa Airlines
2325 E. 30th Street
Farmington, NM 87401
Attn: Personnel
Corporate headquarters # -(505) 327-0271
Sales - $50 million
Employees - 500

Mesaba Aviation, Inc. / Northwest Airlink
Attn: Human Resources
7501 26th Ave. South
Minneapolis, MN 55450
Corporate headquarters # - (612) 726-5151
Job hotline # - (612) 726-5155 ext.2
Fax # - (612) 725-4902 (Can fax resume and cover letter)
Sales - $124 million
Employees - 1,350

Piedmont / USAir Express
5443 Airport Terminal Rd.
Salisbury, MD 21804
Attn: Personnel
Corporate headquarters # - (410) 742-2996
Employees - 1,100

PSA Airlines / US Air Express
3400 Terminal Drive
Vandalia, OH 45377
Attn: Human Resources
Corporate headquarters # - (513) 454-1116
Employees - 761

Skywest Airlines / Delta Connection
444 S. River Rd.
St. George, UT 84790
Corporate headquarters # - (801) 634-3000

Trans States Airlines
4534 Lindbergh Blvd., Suite 540
St. Louis, MO 63044
Corporate headquarters # - (314) 895-8700
Sales - $120 million
Employees - 1,450

Trans World Express
1495 Natural Bridge Rd. Suite 214
St. Louis, MO 63044
Attn: TWTA/TWE
Corporate headquarters # - (314) 589-3000
Flight Attendant Information # - 1-800-942-7467

West Air / United Express
5588 Air Corp Way
Fresno, CA 93727
Attn: Inflight Department
Corporate headquarters # - (209) 294-6915

Job Log

COMPANY	REQUEST APPLICATION	RECEIVED REPLY	APPLICATION SENT	INTERVIEW DATE	REMARKS/CONTACTS

Military Time Conversion Chart

All the airlines function on military time. Below is a chart showing military time in relation to the 24 hour clock. It is important to understand military time as it is used in all aspects of the airline industry such as check-in times, schedules, etc.

Military Time	**24 Hour Clock**
00:00	12:00 AM (Midnight)
01:00	1:00 AM
02:00	2:00 AM
03:00	3:00 AM
04:00	4:00 AM
05:00	5:00 AM
06:00	6:00 AM
07:00	7:00 AM
08:00	8:00 AM
09:00	9:00 AM
10:00	10:00 AM
11:00	11:00 AM
12:00	12:00 PM (Noon)
13:00	1:00 PM
14:00	2:00 PM
15:00	3:00 PM
16:00	4:00 PM
17:00	5:00 PM
18:00	6:00 PM
19:00	7:00 PM
20:00	8:00 PM
21:00	9:00 PM
22:00	10:00 PM
23:00	11:00 PM

The minutes are counted as follows:

5:15 PM in military time is 17:15

3:35 AM in military time is 03:35

12:45 AM in military time is 00:45

11:10 PM in military time is 23:10

Airline City Codes

CAK	Akron, OH	LAX	Los Angeles
ALB	Albany, NY	MEM	Memphis, TN
ABQ	Albuquerque, NM	MIA	Miami, FL
ABE	Allentown, PA	MKE	Milwaukee, WI
AMA	Amarillo, TX	MSP	Minneapolis/St.Paul, MN
ANC	Anchorage, AK	BNA	Nashville, TN
AUS	Austin, TX	MSY	New Orleans, LA
BWI	Baltimore, MD	JFK	New York, NY (Kennedy)
BHM	Birmingham, AL		
BOI	Boise, ID	LGA	New York, NY (LaGuardia)
BOS	Boston, MA		
BUF	Buffalo, NY	OAK	Oakland, CA
BUR	Burbank, CA	OKC	Oklahoma City, OK
CID	Iowa City, IA	OMA	Omaha, NE
CLT	Charlotte, NC	ONT	Ontario, CA
MDW	Chicago, IL (Midway)	SNA	Orange County, CA
		MCO	Orlando, FL
ORD	Chicago, IL (O'Hare)	PHL	Philadelphia, PA
		PHX	Phoenix, AZ
CVG	Cincinnati, OH	PDX	Portland, OR
CLE	Cleveland, OH	PVD	Providence, RI
COS	Colorado Springs, CO	RDU	Raleigh/ Durham, NC
CMH	Columbus, OH	RNO	Reno/Tahoe, NV
DFW	Dallas/Ft.Worth, TX	STL	St. Louis, MO
DAY	Dayton, OH	SAT	San Antonio, TX
DEN	Denver, CO	SAN	San Diego, CA
DTW	Detroit, MI	SFO	San Francisco, CA
EUG	Eugene, OR	SBA	Santa Barbara, CA
FAI	Fairbanks, AK	SEA	Seattle/Tacoma, WA
FAR	Fargo, ND	SUX	Sioux City, IA
FAT	Fresno, CA	TPA	Tampa, FL
GNV	Gainesville, FL	TUS	Tucson, AZ
GRB	Green Bay, WI	TUL	Tulsa, OK
GSO	Greensboro/ Winston Salem, NC	IAD	Washington, DC (Dulles)
MDT	Harrisburg, PA	DCA	Washington, DC (National)
BDL	Hartford, CT		

Fact Sheets On The Major Carriers

Alaska Airlines

CEO, Chairman, & President: John F. Kelly
Headquarters: Seattle, Washington
Hubs: Seattle, Portland, Anchorage

History:

✈ Alaska Airlines began as Mc Gee Airways in 1932, offering service between Anchorage and Bristol Bay, Alaska in a single-engine, three-passenger Stinson.

✈ Over the years, mergers and acquisitions produced changes in the name of the airline and saw business expand throughout Alaska and the Lower 48. The Alaska Airlines name was adopted in 1944.

✈ In 1985, Alaska Air Group (AAG) was formed as a holding company for Alaska Airlines. A year later, the holding company acquired Horizon Air, a Seattle based regional carrier, and Long Beach, California based Jet America Airlines. The latter was merged into Alaska Airlines on October, 1987.

Route Structure:

✈ Alaska Airlines serves 45 cities in Alaska, Washington, Oregon, California, Arizona, Nevada, Mexico, and Russia.

Fleet:

How many: 72
Types: McDonnell Douglas MD-80's, Boeing 737-200's & 400's

Additional Information:

✈ In each of the last 20 years, Alaska Airlines has carried more people between Alaska and the Lower 48 states than any other airline.

✈ Alaska Airlines was ranked the 10th largest carrier in 1993 (measured by revenue passenger miles). It has grown from the 20th spot, which it held during the deregulation era.

✈ In 1993 Alaska Airlines was named the best airline for the fifth straight year by Conde Nast Traveler.

America West Airlines

CEO & Chairman: William A. Franke
Headquarters: Phoenix, Arizona
Hubs: Phoenix, Las Vegas, Columbus (mini-hub)

History

- ✈ America West was founded August 1, 1983 with 3 aircraft and 280 employees.
- ✈ Incorporated in 1981, the carrier is a product of the deregulated airline industry.
- ✈ In 1990 America West achieved major-airline status, with annual revenues of over one billion dollars.

Route Structure:

- ✈ America West flies coast-to-coast including most major destinations. They offer service to 88 domestic destinations in 36 states and District of Columbia including international service to Mexico and Canada.

Fleet:

How Many:	87
Types:	Airbus A320's, Boeing 757's and Boeing 737's
Average Age of Fleet:	9.4 years

Additional Information:

- ✈ America West employees in field stations are cross-utilized which means they are not only trained as a flight attendants but as gate agents and ramp personnel. There is an opportunity to work in all of these capacities.

American Airlines

CEO, Chairman, & President:	Robert L. Crandall
Headquarters:	Dallas/Ft.Worth, Texas
Hubs:	Dallas/Ft. Worth, Raleigh
	Durham, Nashville, Miami

History:

→ American Airlines was founded in 1932.

→ On March 8, 1971 American Airlines merged with Trans Caribbean Airways, Inc.

→ In July 1987 American Airlines merged with AirCal.

→ In 1991 American acquired Trans World Airlines' routes between New York, Los Angeles, and Boston, and London's Heathrow Airport.

Route Structure:

→ American Airlines flies to 170 destinations in North America, Latin America, Europe, the Caribbean, and the Pacific.

Fleet:

How many:	667 jet aircraft
Types:	Airbus A300, Boeing 727's, Boeing 757's, Boeing 767's, McDonnel Douglas DC-10's, McDonnel Douglas MD-11, McDonnel Douglas MD-80's, Fokker 100's

Additional Information:

→ American Airlines is one of the largest scheduled passenger airlines in the world.

→ AMR owns the four American Eagle Airlines (Flagship, Simmons, Executive, and Wings West), which provide turbo-prop service to smaller cities American Airlines does not service.

Continental Airlines

CEO & President: Gordon M. Bethune
Headquarters: Houston, Texas
Hubs: Newark, Cleveland, Houston, Greensborough

History:

+ Founded July 15, 1934 as Varney Speed Lines, which consisted of four pilots and two airplanes flying between Denver-Pueblo-Las Vegas-Santa Fe-Albuquerque-El Paso.
+ Robert F. Six joined the company and became president, a post he would retain for over 40 years. Mr. Six changed the name to Continental Airlines.
+ Provided service in both World War II and Vietnam.
+ In 1982 Continental Airlines and Texas Air Corporation were merged, retaining the Continental identity.
+ Upon the acquisition of Frontier Airlines in 1986 and the integration of People Express and New York Air in 1987, Continental became the third largest carrier in the United States.
+ At the end of 1993, Continental was the fifth largest airline, as measured by revenue passenger miles.

Route Structure:

+ Continental Airlines serves 136 cities throughout the United States and 57 International destinations.

Fleet:

How many: 316 jet aircraft
Types: Boeing 747's, 727's, 737's, McDonnel Douglas DC-10's, DC-9's, MD-80's, Airbus A-300's

Delta Airlines

CEO & Chairman: Ronald W. Allen
Headquarters: Atlanta, Georgia
Hubs: Atlanta, Dallas/Ft.Worth, Cincinnati, Salt Lake City, Los Angeles, and Orlando. Delta has a Pacific hub in Portland, Oregon, an Atlantic hub in New York- John F. Kennedy Airport, and a European hub in Frankfurt, Germany.

History:

✈ Delta Airlines was founded in 1928 in Monroe, Louisiana, as Delta Air Service, a purely agricultural crop dusting company.

✈ Passenger service began in 1929 with 5-passenger Travel Air 6000 aircraft over a route that extended from Dallas, Texas to Jackson, Mississippi.

Route Structure:

✈ Delta currently offers over 2,600 flights each day to 217 cities around the world.

Fleet:

How many: 565 jet aircraft with orders and options for over 250 additional aircraft for delivery in the next 10 years.

Types: Airbus A310's, Boeing 737's, 727's 757's, 767's, 11011's, MD-11's, MD-88's

Avg. age: 4.0 years

Additional Information:

✈ Delta Airlines is the only major carrier whose flight attendants are not members of a union.

✈ For the second time, Delta was named to the Top Ten List in the "100 Best Companies to work for in America" the best selling book by Levering and Koskowitz.

✈ Delta has the best overall record for passenger satisfaction of any major U.S. airline based on statistics compiled by the U.S. Department of Transportation since 1971.

Northwest Airlines

CEO & President: John H. Dasburg
Headquarters: Minneapolis/St.Paul, Minnesota
Hubs: Detroit, Minneapolis/St. Paul, Memphis, Tokyo

History:

→ Northwest began operations in October 1926, flying mail between Minneapolis/ St. Paul and Chicago. They did not begin passenger service until 1927.

→ Northwest pioneered the "Great Circle" or polar route to the Orient and has operated in the Pacific longer than any other U.S. or foreign airline.

→ Acquired Republic Airlines in 1986

Route Structure:

→ Northwest serves more than 275 cities in 19 countries on three continents--Asia, Europe, and North America. In the U.S. Northwest provides service to 43 states and 111 domestic airports.

Fleet:

How many: 386 jet aircraft
Types: Boeing 727's, 747's, 757's, McDonnell Douglas DC-9's, DC10's, and Airbus A320's. Northwest has 60 aircraft on order, including Boeing 747- 400's and 757-200's and Airbus A320's and A330's
Avg. Age: 16.8 years

Additional Information:

→ Northwest is the world's fourth largest airline and America's oldest carrier with continuous name identification.

→ Of Northwest's 43,000 employees, 8,600 are flight attendants.

→ Northwest has flown the Pacific longer than any other U.S. airline and offers the most service of any airline in the U.S.-Japan market.

→ For the fifth consecutive year, Northwest finished first among the seven largest U.S. airlines in domestic on-time performance statistics compiled by the U.S. Department of Transportation.

Southwest Airlines

President, Chairman, and CEO: Herbert D. Kelleher
Headquarters: Dallas/Ft.Worth, Texas

History:

✈   Southwest began customer service on June 18, 1971 as Air Southwest with three Boeing 737 aircraft serving Dallas, Houston and San Antonio. It was founded by Herbert D. Kelleher, the current President and CEO, and Rollin King.

✈   In 1978, deregulation allowed Southwest to expand outside Texas, which they have continued to do for the last 17 years.

Route Structure:

✈   At year end 1994, Southwest provided service to 45 cities in 22 states, mainly in the midwestern, southwestern, and western regions of the U.S

Fleet:

How many: 199 jet aircraft
Types: Boeing 737's
Avg. Age: 7.6 years

Additional Information:

✈   In 1994 Southwest won the their third Triple Crown for best baggage handling, best on-time performance, and fewest customer complaints per customer carried.

✈   Placed first in the Airline Quality Rating Statistics in 1994.

✈   Southwest keeps costs low by offering a limited in-flight service (beverages and peanuts), as well as providing short-haul, low-fare, point-to-point flights.

✈   Rated as one of America's Top Ten companies to work for according to Robert Levering and Milton Moskowitz's 1993 bestseller, "The 100 Best Companies Work for in America".

✈   Southwest offers the best customer service, according to the U.S.Department of Transportation statistics.

Trans World Airlines

President & CEO: Jeffrey H. Erickson
Headquarters: St. Louis, Missouri
Hubs: Domestic - St. Louis, MO
                                     International- New York City, NY

History:

→ TWA was founded in 1925 as Western Air Express.

→ In 1930 Western Air merged with Transcontinental Air Transport and became Transcontinental & Western Air (T&WA)

→ In 1950 the corporate name was changed to Trans World Airlines, Inc.

Route Structure:

→ TWA and TWE (Trans World Express, the airline's network of commuter carriers) serve more than 110 destinations in the United States and Caribbean and 16 cities in Europe and the Middle East.

Fleet:

How many: 192 jet aircraft

Types: McDonnel Douglas DC-9's and MD-80's, Boeing 727's, 747's, 767's, and Lockheed 1011's

Avg. Age: 17.8 years but should be reduced to 10.1 years by December 1997 due to new aircraft on order.

Additional Information:

→ TWA reconfigured coach section of their aircraft for domestic flights, allowing 50% more leg room. Coach is now referred to as "comfort class". This pleases the passengers, as well as the flight attendants as it allows for additional work space and storage space for passengers carry-ons.

United Airlines

Chairman & CEO:	Gerald Greenwald
Headquarters:	Chicago, Illinois
Hubs:	Chicago, Denver, San Francisco, Washington, DC Pacific hub-Tokyo Atlantic hub-London

History:

- ✈ United Airlines began by delivering mail in 1926.
- ✈ United Airlines was a result of four carriers merging; Boeing Air Transport, National Air Transport, Pacific Air Transport, and Varney Air Lines.
- ✈ United Airlines offered the first flight attendant service in 1930.
- ✈ United Airlines had the first non-stop coast-to-coast flight in 1955.
- ✈ United began it's first scheduled service outside North America in 1983 with non-stop service to Tokyo.
- ✈ In 1990, United made it's first flight into Europe with service from Washington DC to Germany.
- ✈ In 1992 United began flying to South America.

Route Structure:

- ✈ Serves a total of 100 domestic and 39 international airports in 30 countries and 3 territories. As well as extensive service in the U.S. they also fly to Latin America, Canada, Europe, Asia, South Pacific, and U.S. Territories.

Fleet:

How many:	549 jet aircraft
Types:	Boeing 727's, 737's, 747's, 757's, 767's, McDonnell Douglas DC-10's, Airbus 320's

Additional Information:

- ✈ United is one of the worlds' largest airlines measured by operating revenues, revenue passengers, and passenger miles flown.
- ✈ Mileage Plus is United's frequent flyer program
- ✈ In 1994 United Airlines successfully implemented an ESOP (Employee Stock Ownership Program) and became the largest company in the world with a majority of its stock owned by employees.

US Air

CEO & Chairman:	Stephen M. Wolf
Headquarters:	Arlington, Virginia
Hubs:	Pittsburgh, Charlotte, Philadelphia, Baltimore

History:

→ U.S. Air began March 5, 1937, as All American Aviation, Inc., changing their name to All American Airways, Inc. in 1948, Allegheny Airlines, Inc. in 1953, and finally to US Air Inc. in 1979.

→ In 1972 US Air merged with Mohawk Airlines, retaining the US Air name.

→ In 1987 US Air acquired Pacific Southwest Airlines and in 1987 acquired Piedmont Aviation.

Route Structure:

→ US Air provides service to 115 cities with 2,270 daily departures. They fly into 41 U.S. States including the District of Columbia, Puerto Rico, U.S. Virgin Islands, Bahamas, Bermuda, Canada, Mexico, Jamaica, Netherlands Antilles, Cayman Islands, Germany, and France.

Fleet:

How many:	416 jet aircraft
Types:	Boeing 767's, 757's, 727'd, 737's, McDonnel Douglas MD 80's, DC-9's
Avg. Age:	10.4 years

Additional Sources Of Information On Carriers

✈ Write/call the particular carrier and ask for a fact sheet and annual report.

✈ Moody's Transportation Manual.

✈ Moody's Standard & Poors for financial information on publicly traded companies.

✈ World Aviation Directory.

✈ Talk to employees of the particular carrier.

Glossary of Abbreviations and Terminology

A - Scale Employee
An airline employee hired before deregulation (1987) that earns a higher wage than B-scale employees, who were hired after deregulation. Typically B-scale employees will merge into A-scale pay rates after a specific period of time.

A/C
Aircraft

AFA
Association Of Flight Attendants

Aft
The rear section of the aircraft

Airstair
Stairs in the rear of some aircraft used for boarding and deplaning.

Aisle Chair
Narrow wheelchair that can fit down the aisle of the aircraft to assist passengers in boarding and deplaning.

Arm Door
Method of engaging the emergency evacuation slide located on the aircraft door.

ATC
Air Traffic Control. The ground-based radio communication facilities responsible for the take-offs, landings, and flight plans of all aircraft.

B - Scale Employee
Airline employee hired after deregulation of the airlines, earning a lower rate of pay than the A-scale employees hired before deregulation.

Base
Also referred to as a domicile. Assigned city out of which a crews trips originate and end.

Bidding
The process of selecting a schedule for the month based on seniority.

Block Time
Measured from the time the aircraft pulls away from the gate at its point of departure until the aircraft pulls into the gate at its point of arrival.

Bulkhead
A partition used to divide the passenger cabin.

Cabin
The interior of the aircraft occupied by passengers.

Cabin Crew
Flight attendants.

Captain
Pilot in command of aircraft and crew.

Coach
The rear most section of the cabin, offering the most economical seats available on the aircraft.

Cockpit
Also referred to as Flight Deck. Forward part of aircraft where cockpit crew works.

Cockpit Crew
Captain, First Officer, Engineer.

Commuter
Someone who lives in another city besides their assigned domicile, and uses their flight benefits to travel to work.

Demo Equipment
Oxygen mask, seat belt, life vest, and safety information card used by flight attendants to do a safety demonstration.

Deregulation
Act passed in 1978 that eliminated government regulation of airline routes and fares.

Disarm Door
Method of disengaging the emergency evacuation slide located on the aircraft door.

Ditching
An emergency water landing.

DOT
Department of Transportation. Government body that regulates the transportation industry. FAA is part of the DOT.

Duty Time
Measured from the time a flight attendant checks in for the day until he/she has had a debriefing and checked out for the day.

Engineer
Pilot third in command.

ETA
Estimated Time of Arrival.

F/A
Flight Attendant

FAA
Federal Aviation Administration. Government body that regulates the airline industry.

FAR
Federal Aviation Regulations. Rules and regulations created by the FAA pertaining to the safety of airline industry.

Ferry Flight
Delivery of aircraft without passengers.

First Class
Most expensive seats available on the aircraft due to the increased customer service, meal/beverage service, leg room, etc.

First Flight Attendant
Flight Attendant responsible for organization and communication between flight attendants and cockpit crew.

First Officer
Second Pilot In Command

Fuselage
Body of the aircraft.

Galley
Area of the aircraft where food and beverages are stored and prepared.

Gate
Area in the airport designated for the arrival and departure of aircraft and passengers.

Grounded
Aircraft not allowed to take-off due to mechanical or other safety related problems.

Holding
Aircraft waiting for clearance from air traffic controllers to take-off or land.

Hub
Cities that an airline has the majority of their departures and arrivals out of.

Jetway
Enclosed walkway between the terminal and aircraft used for boarding and deplaning passengers.

Jumpseat
Seats designated for flight attendants to sit in for take-off and landing, located near exits.

Layover
A scheduled rest for crew members while working a trip.

Lead Flight Attendant
See First Flight Attendant

Leg
One segment of a trip.

Line
Monthly schedule of trips for a crew member.

LOA
Leave Of Absence. Granted from one month to several years, it allows flight attendants and pilots to take time off with out pay to pursue other options, i.e. travel, care for children or elderly parents, etc.

MX
Mechanical.

Narrow Body
Jet aircraft with a single aisle dividing the passenger seats.

No-go Item
Item which is required to be operational for a flight to continue.

Non-Revenue
Airline employee traveling on a pass.

Ops
Operations

Overhead Bins
Storage space above passengers seats to store carry-on items.

Pass
Pleasure travel at a reduced rate for airline employees and their families.

PAX
Passengers.

PBE
Protective Breathing Equipment. Protective hood containing oxygen used by flight attendants when fighting a fire.

Per Diem
Money paid to crew members at an hourly rate for expenses incurred while away on a trip.

Pre-Boarding
Early boarding of passengers who may need additional time or assistance boarding the aircraft.

Reserve
Flight attendants on call.

RON
Remain Overnight. Same as Layover.

Runway
Take-off and landing strip for aircraft.

Second Officer
Flight Engineer.

Space Available
Stand-by travel with no reserved seat.

Sterile Cockpit
Period of time the cockpit may not be disturbed, except for an emergency (Taxi, 10 minutes after take-off or 10 minutes before landing).

Tailwind
Wind blowing in the same direction aircraft is traveling.

UM
Unaccompanied Minor. Child under 12 traveling without an adult.

WX
Weather

Order Form

Fax Orders: (303) 470-2964

Postal Orders: Flight Attendant Corporation Of America
P.O. Box 260803
Littleton, Colorado 80163-9961

Name_____

Address_____

City_____**State**_____**Zip**_____

Telephone (_____**)**_____

Credit Card Orders

Visa ☐   **MasterCard** ☐   **Discover** ☐

Credit Card Number_____

Expiration Date_____

Signature of Cardholder_____

Cost

An Insider's SECRETS To Becoming A Flight Attendant" is only $19.95 plus $4.00 shipping and handling.

Guarantee

If for any reason you are not completely satisfied, please return "An Insider's SECRETS To Becoming A Flight Attendant" for a full refund - no questions asked.